ROBERT WISE
ON HIS FILMS

ROBERT WISE

ON HIS FILMS

FROM

EDITING

ROOM TO

DIRECTOR'S

CHAIR

BY SERGIO LEEMANN

SILMAN-JAMES PRESS
Los Angeles

IN COOPERATION WITH THE DIRECTORS GUILD OF AMERICA

First Edition

10 9 8 7 6 5 4 3 2 1

Library of Congress Cataloging-in-Publication Data

Leemann, Sergio.
Robert Wise on his films : from editing room to director's chair /
by Sergio Leemann.
p. cm.
"In cooperation with the Directors Guild of America."
1. Wise, Robert, 1914- —criticism and interpretation.
2. Wise, Robert, 1914- —Interviews.
I. Directors Guild of America. II. Title.
PN1998.3.W569L44   1995   791.43'0233'092—dc20   95-10963

ISBN: 1-879505-24-X

Cover design by Heidi Frieder

Printed and bound in the United States of America

SILMAN-JAMES PRESS
distributed by
Samuel French Trade
7623 Sunset Blvd.
Hollywood, CA 90046

For Meity

ACKNOWLEDGMENTS

*T*his book was conceived in the mid-1980s to address a major omission in film literature—there were no books about Robert Wise and his films. It seemed to me that the best way to illustrate his long, multiform career was to have Wise himself talk about his experiences. Fortunately, he agreed to what turned out to be the lengthy series of interviews and conversations from which I prepared this book. I couldn't have wished for a more cooperative, kind, patient, and understanding subject. Knowing Robert Wise and working with him on this project has been immensely gratifying for me.

I would like to express my thanks to Ernest Lehman, Saul Chaplin, Nelson Gidding, William Reynolds, and the late Maurice Zuberano for sharing their memories of working with Wise; to Anton Mueller, whose friendship and advice were fundamental in getting this book done; to Ned Comstock for making the University of Southern California's collection of Wise papers available to me; to Tom Bussell, Julia Antopol Hirsch, Albert and Charlotte Sutterlin, Luis Villar, Alvaro Motta, A. C. Gomes de Mattos, Gil Araujo, Wayne T. Santos, Francisco Sergio Moreira, Cecilia Mello Flores, and Mauricio Lemus for their inestimable help.

This book would not have been possible without the invaluable assistance of the Directors Guild of America, especially Selise E. Eiseman, DGA's National Special Projects Officer, and Adele Field, DGA's Oral History Editor.

To Pio, Vera, Jose Eduardo, Roberto, and Denise Giraldez, my most heartfelt thanks for your generosity and love.

Contents

FOREWORD
by ARTHUR HILLER

A four-time Oscar winner.

A world-renowned producer-director of films. (Can you name one country in the world where they don't sing songs from *The Sound of Music*?)

A father figure to so many of us in the film industry.

Recipient of the Directors Guild of America Award for Outstanding Achievements and Lifetime Contribution to Film and the Academy of Motion Picture Arts and Sciences Award for Lifetime Achievement in Film.

Boy, what more can there be about this legendary director?

Well . . .

How many acclaimed directors can say they have received literally dozens of tributes from international film festivals and universities around the world (not to mention honorary degrees)?

How many can say they have given seminars for film students at over twenty universities and colleges?

How many can say they have mentored hundreds of young filmmakers?

How many can say they have been President of both the Directors Guild of America and the Academy of Motion Picture Arts and Sciences and been Chairman of the American Film Institute Center for Advanced Film Studies?

How many can say they have received the National Medal of the Arts from the President of the United States or the Grand Decoration of Honor for Services to the Republic of Austria or Knight in the Order of Leopold from the King of Belgium?

And that's just for starters.

Robert Wise is a major contributor to hundreds and hundreds of charities and needy arts organizations, be they local or traveling—struggling theater groups or dance companies or music groups or museums or any other organization that gives us or preserves our cultural heritage . . . and I'm not even talking about what a wonderful and caring human being he is. Bob really cares about a fair and wonderful world, moral values, and the rights of artists . . . and not only does he care, he does something about it. Bob is the definition of "one of a kind."

It would be such a gain for all of us if we had more Robert Wises in the world.

—Arthur Hiller

FOREWORD
by NELSON GIDDING

This year, at a film festival in Istanbul, Robert Wise celebrated sixty-two years in the film industry. This same year, the movie *Forrest Gump* won the Academy Award for Best Picture and the book *Gumpisms* has just been published. The best-known Gumpism is about life being like a box of chocolates.

Here's a Wiseism of equal sagacity: "I don't want to be the first to be second."

That was his response to being asked to do a remake. Perhaps it explains why Bob Wise is first in many things. Even so, his modesty is monumental.

One of his strengths is that he doesn't repeat himself in his life or his movies. The range of his work is wide. He can't be categorized in any particular genre. He has directed distinguished films of every kind, from horror to musicals. He prefers movies that say something without *saying* it.

Of the pictures I've worked on with him, I think his passion was *I Want to Live!* The way he shot the gas chamber, which was recreated with rivet-for-rivet exactitude, reflected his deep opposition to the death penalty. Mine, as well.

On two other pictures I wrote for him, we started out with different points of view. Before he made *The Haunting*, Bob had trouble accepting the supernatural. The location was a rural hotel equipped with a private ghost of its own. For budgetary reasons, Bob used him—her? it?—as an extra. The inexpensive private ghost convinced him, at least, to accept the supernatural, meaning events that can't be explained now, but in the future will have a scientific explanation.

The Haunting is a genuine ghost story. The house is honestly haunted. No cop-outs. Bob didn't waffle or blink. He never does.

I blinked. Halfway through the script, I began to think that Jackson's novel wasn't a ghost story at all. We had missed the point of the book. It's about a mental institution, a private sanitarium, where the heroine, Eleanor, is confined. What could be more obvious?

The doors in the house mysteriously open and close as they would appear to a sensitive, disturbed person, like Eleanor, in a locked facility. Dr. Markway, the professor conducting an experiment in the supernatural, is, of course, the medical doctor in charge of the institution.

Eleanor's lesbian friend, Theo, is a fellow patient. Mrs. Markway, who appears disastrously at the end, is the head nurse; the cavalier Luke, a male nurse. The terrifying noises that Eleanor hears in her head are the result of medication. The thunderous bangings and explosions emphasize the violence of the shock treatment that Eleanor is undergoing. The cold spot and freezing sensation that Eleanor feels on occasion are the aftereffects of shock treatment.

No doubt about it, we had misunderstood the book. Bob decided we must fly posthaste to Shirley Jackson in Bennington, Vermont, and ask her if, indeed, Hill House was supposed to be a sanitarium for the mentally ill rather than a haunted house. Over lunch with her, I cited all my reasons for thinking this.

Shirley Jackson said, no, that wasn't at all what she meant, but it was a damn good idea. Much relieved, we continued with our no-holds-barred, honest-to-God ghost story.

Another of Bob's projects that we approached from different perspectives is *The Andromeda Strain*. Bob is drawn to the rational and factual elements in science fiction. I prefer the fanciful side. He regarded *Andromeda* in terms of science fact rather than sci-fi. The extensive bibliography at the end of Michael Crichton's book confirmed Bob's belief in its scientific accuracy. Three pages of "unclassified documents, reports, and references" list such items as:

Merrick, J.J. "Frequencies of Biologic Contact According to Speciation Probabilities," *Proceedings of the Cold Springs Harbor Symposia* 10:443-57.

Having less faith in the scientific credentials of his screenwriter, Bob engaged a team of advisors from the Jet Propulsion Laboratory in Pasadena to ride shotgun. I found their advice and infrequent consent stifling. Bob insisted that I continue to walk the straight and narrow with them. One morning, during a painful meeting in his office, he finally came to my defense. He admonished the experts that their job was to show me a way to make my inspirations plausible and not to keep shooting them down.

"The problem is," said Doctor Green, the top advisor, "that Crichton has placed the satellite's orbit only 317 miles above the earth. If you put it in deep space, almost anything is possible."

Deep space it was—and still is. Later, while checking on an article listed in the bibliography, I discovered that the entire bibliography is fictional, created by Crichton's brash and vivid imagination.

It was a pleasure to tell this to Bob, but only a minor one among the many I've had knowing him over the years. I might mention his total honesty, unbending integrity, humanity . . . I'd better stop here.

Bob Wise hates effusiveness. I won't even say thanks.

—Nelson Gidding

OVERVIEW

2034-63

*Wise on location for **The Sand Pebbles**.*

*I*t was the height of the Great Depression. Just three months before he turned nineteen, Robert Wise's parents informed him that they no longer could afford to keep him in college and that he had to go to Los Angeles and find himself a job. That was a serious blow to the studious young man who dreamed of becoming a journalist, but his acute disappointment was partially offset by the prospect of moving to a new environment. This unexpected change in the course of his life would in time lead Wise to his true vocation and to his attaining a prominence in the ranks of American filmmakers that went beyond any aspirations he might have had when he first arrived in Hollywood.

Wise is a remarkable example of the director who learned his craft from the ground up. He started his gradual advancement by carrying prints at the RKO Studios. After years of training in the sound and film-editing departments, he was promoted to full-fledged film editor. Among his dozen credits in that capacity was the epochal *Citizen Kane* [1941], which earned him an Oscar nomination. Directing was the natural next step up the ladder for the determined Wise. His opportunity came when he was chosen to replace the original director of *The Curse of the Cat People* [1944] halfway through filming. Like any novice cutting his teeth at the time, Wise's initial directorial chores were B-films, among which figures the impressive *The Body Snatcher* [1945]. In 1948, Wise ascended to more important productions with the brooding western noir *Blood on the Moon*, and he closed the decade and his long tenure at RKO with the masterful *The Set-Up* [1949].

Wise belongs to the last generation of directors trained under the studio system. Although some of his contemporaries shared his penchant for flexing his muscles on every established movie genre, Wise infused his output with a protean quality. Never was his versatility more pronounced than in the 1950s, when his seemingly insatiable appetite for expanding his repertoire and sharpening his technique yielded eighteen features. There were a few assignments he took on reluctantly, but the decade brought forth several solid films, such as the melodramas *Three*

Secrets [1950] and *So Big* [1953], the war adventure *The Desert Rats* [1953], the western *Tribute to a Bad Man* [1956], the comedy *This Could Be the Night* [1957], and the submarine drama *Run Silent, Run Deep* [1958].

Wise's reputation during that period, however, derived from a group of crisply realistic, socially conscious films in which critics saw confirmed the expectations raised by *The Set-Up*. In tackling some of the relevant issues of our time, Wise revealed himself an impassioned humanist who put his considerable skills at the service of engaging and enlightening his

audience within the framework of the entertainment film. The cautionary science-fiction thriller *The Day the Earth Stood Still* [1951] warned about the dangers of nuclear armament; the all-star drama *Executive Suite* [1954] dealt with the responsibilities of big business; the biographical *Somebody Up There Likes Me* [1956] showed how a man can overcome the overwhelming limitations of his milieu; the harrowing *I Want to Live!* [1958] attacked capital punishment with uncompromising candor; the caper *Odds Against Tomorrow* [1959] demonstrated the destructive power of racial hatred.

All of the above-mentioned were films offered to Wise either by the studios with which he was affiliated or by independent producers, and it was his good fortune to be able to make films that so closely mirrored his own personal views, despite the fact that he did not initiate the projects himself. Nevertheless, Wise yearned to gain more autonomy. His first bid toward independence happened as far back as 1949, when he formed a production company, Aspen, for which he was able to make only one film, the semi-documentary thriller *The Captive City* [1952]. After leaving MGM in 1957, Wise vowed not to be tied to a studio again by a long-term contract. The artistic and commercial success of *I Want to Live!* gave him the clout to join that exclusive Hollywood fraternity of producer-directors that emerged in the late '50s and included the likes of Elia Kazan, Fred Zinnemann, Richard Brooks, and Billy Wilder.

Wise reached the pinnacle of his prestige in the industry over the next two decades. He continued to work as hard as before, but his participation in every phase of his productions, from selecting their stories to overseeing their release, coupled with his involvement in big-budget, high-profile films, entailed a sharp decrease in his output—only eleven features in twenty years. The '60s were the heyday of the roadshows—long, expensive films released on a reserved-seat basis. Every major talent in Hollywood tried his hand at roadshows, but nobody as consistently as Wise, who made four of those spectaculars: *West Side Story* [1961], *The Sound of Music* [1965], *The Sand Pebbles* [1966], and *STAR!* [1968]. The first two became multi-Academy Award winners, with Wise himself collecting a pair of Oscars for each. *The Sound of Music* had the added distinction of breaking all previous box-office records. In the '70s, Wise achieved an even balance between large and small, with each high-priced film (*The Andromeda Strain* [1971], *The Hindenburg* [1975]) followed by a much less costly counterpart (*Two People* [1973], *Audrey Rose* [1977]).

The release of Wise's most popular films coincided with the introduction of the director-as-auteur theory that came to dominate film criticism for many years. Wise never made it to the theoreticians' pantheon of star directors. His work was too heterogeneous in form and content for even the most enterprising among them to discern any repeated patterns that might qualify him as an auteur. Besides, in their view he had abdicated from the trenchant social dramas of the past in favor of lavish escapist fare. Perhaps Wise could have won over his critics if he had aggressively projected an image of himself that would have made clear that the confounding diversity of his films, which at the time included an unpremeditated incidence of expensive musicals, was a natural manifestation of his personality. However, the myriad interviewers who met him back then—as throughout his career—were invariably surprised to find him the very antithesis of the ingrained image of a powerful Hollywood director. He was articulate, soft-spoken, devoid of pretension. Given the countless opportunities he had for self-promotion, Wise made his work and not his personality the focus of attention.

Wise is not the author of his films the way an Ingmar Bergman or a Federico Fellini is. He is a film storyteller par excellence; one who translates into purely cinematic terms the stories of others that he makes his own. In their variety, the scripts Wise has filmed reflect his curious, inquiring nature as well as the hopes and concerns of a man keenly interested in the human condition and the world around him. "Even though I don't make so-called personal films," Wise explains, "they are personal to me in what they express about matters I feel very strongly about, such as social justice, equality, and the need for tolerance. I'm not a man who has just one theme to express through his art. I have different interests and I like to try different things. My first reaction when reading a piece of material is if it grabs me as a reader. The second thought is if there's an audience for it. The third is what is the theme, or the by-product, as I always call it. I hesitate to use the word 'message' because that sounds like a soap box. I feel that whatever the filmmaker has to say in a film should come out strictly in terms of the

Paul Newman, cinematographer Joseph Ruttenberg, Pier Angeli, and Wise on the set of **Somebody Up There Likes Me**.

story itself and the characters. I'm very careful not to do scripts in which you talk about what the message is."

Be it social commentary or out-and-out entertainment, every Robert Wise film displays an uncommonly high degree of craftsmanship. Wise's goal has always been to adapt his style to the demands of screenplays that challenge his ability to communicate cinematically, and it is a testament to his unmatched technical adroitness that each of his films received a visual treatment all its own. "I've been taken apart sometimes for not having a really consistent style," Wise muses, "but that's exactly what I wanted. I try to address each script in the cinematic fashion I think is right for that given script, and since I've done such different kinds of stories, there's no straight stylistic line in my work."

Wise's quest for a distinctive visual presentation for each of his films is made clear in the way he chooses his cinematographers. Unlike most directors, he never had any ongoing collaboration with a cameraman, preferring to hire the photographer for his ability to deliver the particular look that Wise had in mind. Even in his days as a contract director, when the decisions regarding technical personnel were ultimately the department heads', Wise made sure that his concepts were carried out to the letter. For instance, MGM assigned Joseph Ruttenberg, a veteran renowned for the glossy lighting so characteristic of that studio's product, to shoot *Somebody Up There Likes Me*. Wise had envisioned a grainy, documentary-like texture for this gritty story of boxer Rocky Graziano and elected to use Tri-X black-and-white film. Ruttenberg resisted the idea at first, but Wise prevailed and the photographer wound up winning an Oscar. When the two teamed up again for the romantic drama *Until They Sail* [1957], Wise requested a much slicker look, which Ruttenberg was only too happy to provide.

If, visually and thematically, Wise's films vary tremendously, his dedicated, meticulous approach to filmmaking has remained unchanged through the years. Wise is a stickler for realism who will go to any lengths to ensure that there is not a false note in his films. Much of his pre-production time is spent on painstakingly researching the subject, uncovering every nuance that might substantiate the sense of credibility that he will create for the camera. This sort of diligent preparation, combined with his complete knowledge of all aspects of film production and his unrelenting determination to get the very best values on the screen, earned Wise a just reputation as a perfectionist, as well as the respect and admiration of the people he works with. Having come from the technical ranks himself, Wise understands like few directors the collaborative nature of the medium, constantly encouraging the input of his cast and crew.

When he made the transition from editing to directing, Wise realized that being with live actors on the set was completely different from handling their filmed performances on the Moviola. He quickly learned that it was not necessary to give them too many specific directions. "Because a film is shot out of continuity," Wise explains, "the director has to keep the building of the script and the characters in the forefront of his mind at all times to remind the actors where they are in the story when a scene is being shot. Once they have an understanding of the sequence itself and what it adds to the story, I let them discover for themselves. They always find added little dimensions and values that you as the director can't anticipate. I try to incorporate all those that are good. Sometimes they try things that are not good, so you keep molding and developing the scene until you feel it's right. The director's role is almost like a critic's. You're there sitting and judging as an audience, responding to what the actors are giving you."

When planning and shooting a sequence, Wise thinks not only of how he is going to stage it but also how it will be enhanced in post-production. The main distinguishing trait of Wise's style as a director is his extraordinarily lucid sense of rhythm, an outgrowth, no doubt, of his many years as an editor. The arrangement of shots within scenes and the strict correspondence between sequences are of such symmetry and purpose that his films are veritable textbooks on the possibilities of film editing. In 1977, *Film Comment* magazine conducted a poll among 100 film editors from the United States and Europe, asking them to choose the directors who consistently have outstanding editing in their films. Only David Lean, himself a former editor, received more votes than Wise. On the same survey, Wise was named one of the all-time finest editors. "Most people think that because you've been an editor, you don't shoot too much because you know exactly what you're going to need. In my case, I found that because I'd been an editor I know how valuable it is to have extra coverage; so I actually tend to shoot more film. There is almost no limit to what you can do to film in the cutting room."

Wise always felt an obligation to get the audience engrossed in his films in such a way that "they can never escape." As his career progressed, he became increasingly sophisticated in manipulating the viewers' emotions through the use of editing techniques. His early films already contain passages of a remarkable visual nature, but it is with *The Set-Up* that Wise makes his first bold experiment with screen narrative, telling seventy-two minutes in the life of a fading boxer in real time—every minute of screen time being a minute of actual time. Years later, he structured *Executive Suite* almost entirely without dissolves and fade-outs, making an exciting film that in other hands could have become stodgy. Wise elaborated on this approach in *Somebody Up There Likes Me*, where he compressed Rocky Graziano's early life as a juvenile delinquent in a half hour of straight cuts with a swift pace that he maintained until the end of the two-hour film.

But as Wise points out, "Pace is not necessarily speed, pace is interest." *I Want to Live!* proves that notion conclusively. Rhythmically, the film is divided into three separate sections, each markedly slower than the preceding one. As in *Somebody Up There Likes Me*, Wise opens the film with a dynamic condensation of Barbara Graham's shady activities leading up to her arrest. During her ordeal in prison, he adopts a more measured tempo. In the epilogue, as the clinically detailed preparations for her execution in the gas chamber take place, he intensifies Graham's suffering by making the proceedings agonizingly slow.

Wise with Robert Ryan and Audrey Totter during the filming of **The Set-Up**.

On Wise's first day as a director, Richard Wallace, for whom he had edited *Bombardier* [1943] and *The Fallen Sparrow* [1943], stopped by the set to wish him luck in his new career. The veteran director had one piece of advice to the newcomer: "If a scene seems a trifle slow on the set, it will be twice as slow in the projection room." Wise took the counsel to heart: "We all have a tendency to want to milk a good, strong sequence for everything that's in it. But very frequently, when you get that sequence down in reel five, with four reels ahead of it, it will be a little slow. I don't think I could ever remember wishing I had played a sequence slower than I had. If anything, I wish I'd picked up the tempo a little because that sequence is not isolated. You have accumulated a lot of sequences up to the point where the new sequence appears, and they have a bearing and an influence on the film."

The qualities one finds in Robert Wise the man—honesty, integrity, generosity of spirit—are the same that inform a body of work that celebrates the human experience in all its diversity. In answering an inquiry from a French publication in 1987 on why he makes films, Wise responded: "I make films because movies have been a major part of my life for over fifty years. I have become increasingly aware of the power of film as a truly international language. Films can be such a positive force in the world to bring more knowledge and understanding between nations and peoples. I continue to make films in order to aid in bringing the world closer to peace."

1972 lunch at George Cukor's house to honor Luis Buñuel. Top: Robert Mulligan, William Wyler, George Cukor, Robert Wise, Jean-Claude Carrière, Serge Silberman. Bottom: Billy Wilder, George Stevens, Luis Buñuel, Alfred Hitchcock, Rouben Mamoulian.

[following pages] Wise with John Ford.

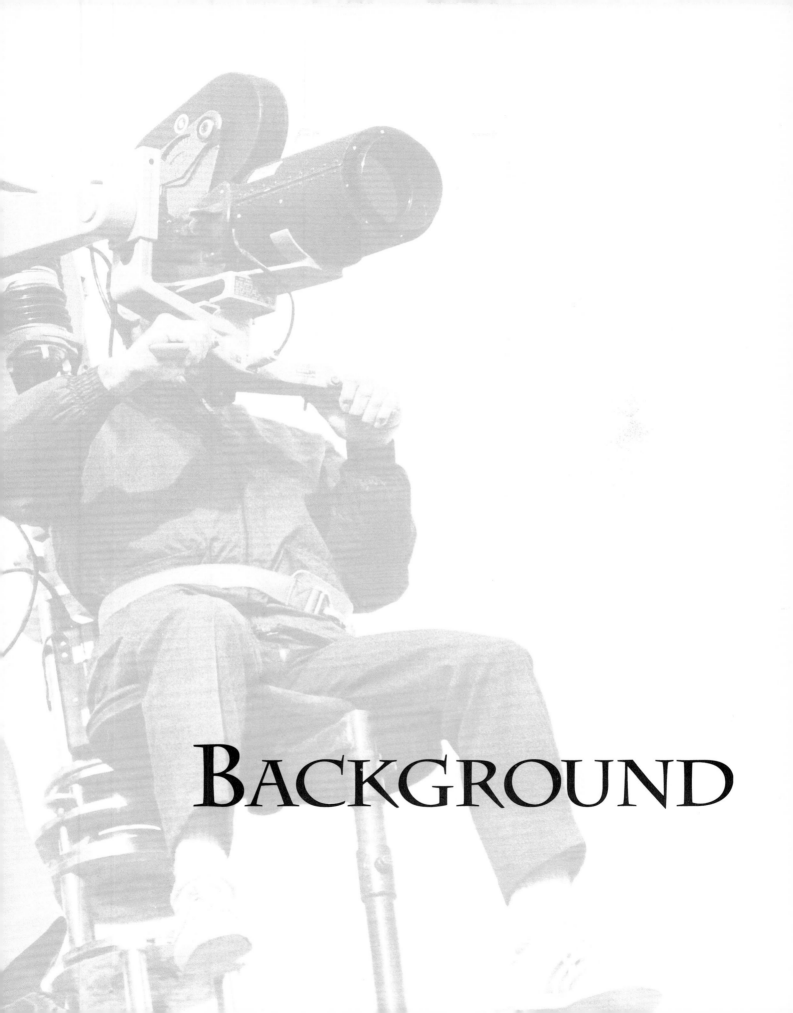

BACKGROUND

Connersville, Indiana, Junior High School Glee Club (c. 1928). Wise is in the front row, third from the left.

Robert Wise was born September 10, 1914, in the small town of Winchester, Indiana, the youngest of three brothers. He was still in grade school when his father moved the family to nearby Connersville to open a new business. With growing economic troubles at home, one of Wise's siblings, David, headed for Los Angeles in 1928, landing a job on the labor gang at the RKO Studios, where he made his way into the accounting office. Wise, in the meantime, graduated from high school and, with the aid of a small scholarship and some money saved by his mother, went off to Franklin College near Indianapolis. After only a year, the family's declining financial state prevented Wise from continuing his studies.

When David came home for a visit in the summer of 1933, his first since he had left five years earlier, it was decided that Robert would return with him to Los Angeles to find a job and earn his living. The brothers arrived in Los Angeles in July and, within a month, David managed to get Robert some interviews with department heads at RKO. One of these was Jimmy Wilkinson, head of the film-editing department. As fate would have it, Wilkinson just happened to need a film porter to carry prints up to the projection booths for the executives to watch, and to check them afterward for damage. Wise was hired at a salary of twenty-five dollars a week.

An avid moviegoer since childhood, Wise was overwhelmed by the hustle and bustle around the RKO lot. His first trip to the studio made a lasting impression on him. "I was a little kid from the middle of Indiana, my eyes were like saucers. I took advantage of the fact that I got inside for the interview just to walk around the studio. I was walking by one of the office buildings when I saw a rather heavy-set fellow with dark, curly hair and thick glasses, dressed in a white shirt and white ducks, talking very animatedly to a couple of ladies in long hoop skirts, underneath parasols. I remember going by and panning my head to watch them, wondering who they were. I described the scene later to somebody who

*Wise, brother David, mother, nephew Jim Wise,
brother Lloyd, father.*

*Wise with his mother in
Connersville (c. 1930).*

said, 'That must have been George
Cukor talking maybe to Katharine
Hepburn and Joan Bennett.' They
were making *Little Women* then.
Many years later, when I got to
know George, I described the scene
to him and said, 'You know George,
you're the first live movie director I
ever saw.'"

Wise had worked in the film
shipping room for seven months
when he caught the attention of T.
K. Wood, the head sound-effects
editor at the studio. Wood recognized Wise as eager and
hardworking, and asked him to join
his department as an apprentice
sound editor. Once there, Wise developed an indispensable requisite
for a future director—the ability to
keep going tirelessly for long
stretches of time. During the first
quarter of the year, the busiest for
the post-production departments,
Wise would work three months in
a row, seven days a week, twelve
to fourteen hours a day. In some
instances, he would literally toil
around the clock. At one point, he
spent two and a half days straight,
with only two hours of sleep, preparing *Alice Adams* [1935], George
Stevens' first important feature as a
director, for a sneak preview.

Following their initial period
working together, Wood suggested
to Wise that they use their spare
time to tinker with some cans of

*Joan Bennett and Katharine Hepburn in **Little Women**.*

George Cukor, Mae West, and Wise at USC tribute to West.

film that Wood had found in a vault. They contained picturesque dailies
shot by Ernest B. Schoedsack in the South Pacific for insertion in a feature that never materialized. With the go-ahead from the studio, the two
men labored on and off for over a year and came up with a short subject called *A Trip Through Fijiland* [1935]. The studio showed its gratitude with a $500. bonus for each, and Wise received his first screen credit
(for the story).

In his two years as Wood's protégé, Wise learned both sound and music editing. When he realized that, beyond being an expert technician, there was little else that unit could offer him creatively, he expressed a wish to move into film editing, and Jimmy Wilkinson assigned him as an assistant to William Hamilton. The seasoned editor took Wise under his wing in much the same way as T. K. Wood had. To Wise's astonishment, his new mentor solicited his input starting with their very first film together, *Winterset* [1936]. Soon, Hamilton came to rely more and more on his apprentice, to the extent that Wise would do all the first cutting himself. Finally, Wise was doing so much of the work that Hamilton insisted that they share the editing credit on *The Hunchback of Notre Dame* [1939] and *Fifth Avenue Girl* [1939].

When Wise went solo, Mark Robson was assigned as his assistant, and their association laid the foundation for a lifelong friendship. After the completion of each film, Wise and Robson would ship the negative to New York for printing and go out to celebrate over dinner. They had just dispatched Garson Kanin's *My Favorite Wife* [1940] when Wise received a call from Jimmy Wilkinson. A brilliant new talent with only a stage and radio background had arrived at the studio and begun shooting a film under the guise of making screen tests. By the time the executives realized what was happening, significant scenes from the film were already in the can, and they reluctantly gave the neophyte director the green flag to finish the project. His name was Orson Welles and he was unhappy with the unimaginative old-time editor assigned to him by the studio. Wise and Welles were about the same age, and after the two met between shots at the Pathé Studios in Culver City, Wise was put in charge of editing *Citizen Kane* [1941].

It wasn't long before Wise recognized that this was no ordinary job; that he had, in fact, become part of something unique. Contrary to what one might expect, in view of Welles' reputation for overseeing every aspect of his productions, Wise recalls no interference. As with all the directors he worked for, Wise would do a first cut on any given scene the way he judged best. Only after Welles had seen Wise's version

Citizen Kane: *Orson Welles and Ruth Warrick in the breakfast-table scene.*

would the director tell his editor what changes he wanted effected. A salient example of Wise's contribution to *Citizen Kane* is the fabled breakfast-table sequence that shows the gradual disintegration of a marriage through a number of short, time-spanning scenes between Kane and his first wife. The overall concept was, of course, Welles', but the prodigious rhythm was achieved on the Moviola. Wise and Robson spent several weeks going back to the sequence until they perfected the speed of the whip-pans and the timing of the incoming voices in each new segment.

Wise's next picture was another of 1941's enduring classics, *All That Money Can Buy* (a.k.a. *The Devil and Daniel Webster*). Its producer-director, William Dieterle, was so impressed with his editor that, when he began preparing his next film, *Syncopation* [1942], he requested Wise's services. At the same time, Orson Welles counted on having Wise as a member of his staff for the film version of Booth Tarkington's *The Magnificent Ambersons* [1942]. The tug of war between the two directors ended with Welles' victory. Unfortunately, *The Magnificent Ambersons* proved to be a much less rewarding experience for Wise than *Citizen Kane*. Welles left for Brazil shortly after shooting wrapped, and Wise saw himself in the uncomfortable position of only having contact with his director via long-distance calls and telegrams. With the film finished, a preview was arranged. It proved disastrous, with the audience laughing at certain passages and walking out of the theater. Fearing the worst, studio executives ordered trimmings, which, consequently, called for some additional bridging scenes to be shot, one of them by Wise himself. Welles was the only person who could have fought the studio's commands. Since he was not around, Wise had to comply, and a greatly altered version of *The Magnificent Ambersons* was ultimately released.

Much has been written about how the professional alliance with Welles affected Wise's style as a director. Wise himself estimates that Welles' influence was much less pervasive than is generally assumed. "Because of the strength of Orson's personality, people imagine that he had more of an influence on me than he actually had. But there were a few things that I'm sure I learned from him. One was to try and keep the energy level high, the movement forward in the telling of the story. Another was the use of deep-focus photography. I've shot many of my films, particularly in black and white, with wide-angle lenses, so we could have somebody close in the foreground and still have things in the background in focus. I'm sure that came from Orson. Also, even though I had been a sound-effects and music editor, I think Orson increased my sense of what a soundtrack contributes to a picture, both in sound effects and in music. Having come from radio, that was something very important to Orson, and my knowledge in that area was certainly heightened by my working with him."

In 1943, Wise edited three popular RKO releases: *Bombardier, The Iron Major*, and *The Fallen Sparrow*. To the latter he also contributed a short sequence with John Garfield that he directed in the absence of director Richard Wallace. Inserts like that and the one in *The Magnificent Ambersons* gave Wise enough of a taste of directing that he felt he was ready to move behind the camera. Wise's insistent requests for an opportunity paid off when Gunther von Fritsch fell seriously behind schedule on the Val Lewton production of *The Curse of the Cat People* [1944], and Wise was asked to step in and bring the project under control.

Val Lewton had served as David O. Selznick's story editor for several years prior to being hired by RKO in 1942 to produce a series of low-budget psychological thrillers. Eschewing the conventional horror formula of mad scientists and gruesome monsters, Lewton set a new standard for the genre with literate and subtle explorations into man's fear of the unknown. The cycle was auspiciously launched with *Cat People* [1942], and continued with *I Walked with a Zombie* [1943] and *The Leopard Man* [1943]. All three were directed by Jacques Tourneur, with whom Lewton had worked on the second unit of Selznick's *A Tale of Two Cities* [1935]. When Tourneur moved on to bigger films, Wise's former assistant Mark Robson, who had edited the Tourneur entries, was put at the helm of *The Seventh Victim* [1943], the first of Robson's five films for Lewton.

RKO wanted to capitalize on the popularity of *Cat People*, and Lewton was told by his bosses to come up with a similar film to be called *The Curse of the Cat People*. The producer resisted the idea for some time, but wound up devising the story of a lonely six-year-old girl and her retreat into a world of make-believe. In order to accommodate the main characters from the previous film, Lewton made little Amy (Ann Carter) the offspring of Oliver (Kent Smith) and Alice Reed (Jane Randolph), who married after the death of Oliver's first wife, Irena (Simone Simon), the cat woman of the original. In the sequel, Irena is Amy's imaginary companion.

Since Mark Robson was occupied with *The Ghost Ship* [1943], Lewton selected Gunther von Fritsch—like Tourneur, a former member of the MGM short-subject department—to direct *The Curse of the Cat People*. It was von Fritsch's first feature and he proved to be a slow director, spending the whole of his twenty-day schedule shooting only half the screenplay. With concern over budget growing in the RKO management, Lewton decided that a change was necessary to save the film. Wise's years of discipline in the cutting room, coupled with the fact that he had been on the set a number of times, served him well; he completed the film in ten days. When *The Curse of the Cat People* opened in March of 1944, it took both critics and audiences by surprise, for the lurid title and promotional campaign could not hide a tender and haunting depiction of the fears and anxieties of childhood. "It's a very sensitive tale, not a scary one," says Wise. "We had some runnings for teachers and child psychologists, and, almost unanimously, they loved the film. But they kept saying, 'What's it

Wise, Val Lewton, and Mark Robson.

doing with that awful title?' That's what started it—the studio wanted a film to go with that title."

If *The Curse of the Cat People* turned out to be something of a departure from Lewton's trademark subliminal thrillers, his next two productions, the juvenile-delinquency drama *Youth Runs Wild* [1944] and the costumer *Mademoiselle Fifi* [1944], had no connection to the genre whatsoever. The latter, Wise's first solo directorial venture, derives from two stories by Guy de Maupassant—"Boule de Suif" (itself the basis for many films, including John Ford's *Stagecoach* [1939]) and "Mademoiselle Fifi." It draws deliberate parallels between the Prussian-occupied France of 1870 and the Nazi-invaded France of the 1940s, praising the virtues of the simple people who remain true to their national pride and condemning those who connive with the enemy for personal gain. The story of the laundress (Simone Simon) who sacrifices her principles to save the other passengers with whom she is traveling on a coach gave Wise the opportunity to tackle an issue seldom seen in films—the role of the middle class in wartime. As a result of the care and dedication with which it was made, *Mademoiselle Fifi* stands out as a brave stab at making a historical film on a shoestring.

This ability to evoke times past with meager resources is displayed again in Wise's final film for Lewton, *The Body Snatcher* [1945]. Taking a Robert Louis Stevenson story about grave robbing in 1860s Edinburgh as the source for his script, Lewton (who received co-writing credit under the pseudonym Carlos Keith) provided Wise with a richly textured meditation on the nature of good and evil that allowed for a character study of some resonance. Henry Daniell as MacFarland, a surgeon who buys corpses for research purposes, and Boris Karloff as Gray, the cynical cab driver who supplies the bodies, are both superb, and their many charged confrontations rank among the best in Wise's work, the superior acting enhanced by the director's inspired staging and editing.

Apart from the interpretive duel, it is moments of genuine terror, ranging from the implied to the explicit, that earned *The Body Snatcher* its status as a minor classic. In a typically subtle one, we see a blind street singer as she walks into a dark passageway. Seconds later, she is followed by Gray's carriage. The camera remains stationary, and only the abrupt stop of the girl's singing tells us of her unfortunate end. In another, as Gray kills MacFarland's servant, played by Bela Lugosi, Wise cuts to a cat that witnesses the violence. But the scene most indelibly etched in the memories of those who saw *The Body Snatcher* is the terrifying climax. After having killed Gray, MacFarland steals the freshly buried body of a

woman so that he can resume his experiments. On the way back from the graveyard, a storm breaks out and, in a state of hallucination, the physician imagines that the body he transports is Gray's and that the cabman is attacking him. Wise directed the delirious night ride for maximum effect, with bolts of lightning and the sounds of rain, galloping horses, and Gray's menacing voice adding to its grisly effect.

The Lewton unit, affectionately known as "The Snake Pit," was dissolved after Mark Robson's *Bedlam* [1946]. Despite the good notices he received for *The Body Snatcher*, Wise found himself restricted to a few run-of-the-mill B-films for the coming two years. *A Game of Death* [1945] was a remake of an earlier RKO hit, *The Most Dangerous Game* [1932], in which the Russian madman who hunts people on a secluded island was conveniently transformed into a Nazi fanatic. It was a film Wise was uncomfortable with

from the outset, but his contract gave him little choice. The same applied to *Criminal Court* [1946], a fast-paced thriller with a convoluted storyline. It is a tribute to Wise's solid training in economical filmmaking that he was able to tell the sinuous story of a politically ambitious attorney (Tom Conway) trying to save his fiancée (Martha O'Driscoll) from a murder charge in just one hour and three minutes.

Things looked better with the next project, one that Wise himself got off the ground. Searching through the story files at RKO one day, he came across a book called *Deadlier Than the Male.* He liked its intricate plot of a predatory woman's attraction to a psychopathic killer and took it to the front office. The studio also saw promise in the material, especially as a vehicle for tough-guy Lawrence Tierney, and gave Wise a larger budget and longer schedule than he had had in the past. The result was an uncommonly rough film noir that tested the boundaries of the Production Code with its amoral characters, sexual innuendo, and sharp outbursts of violence. *Born to Kill,* as the film was eventually christened, provoked mostly indignant reactions from reviewers in 1947. "Shoddy," "offensive," and "morally disgusting," were some of the adjectives that greeted its arrival. The film is most unusual for Wise in that the characters have no redeeming qualities, but he relished in building a palpable mood of seediness and inexorable doom that has gained the film many devotees in recent years.

On location for **Mystery in Mexico**: Wise, assistant director Jaime Contreras, and noted Mexican director Miguel Delgado.

Mystery in Mexico [1948] was another studio assignment over which Wise had no choice. It was a pilot program by RKO to determine the feasibility of making films south of the border for less money than they cost at home. The nominal producer, RKO executive Sid Rogell, accompanied Wise only to get preparations under way, and then left the director on his own to shoot the film in and around Mexico City and Cuernavaca. All in all, Wise spent four months in Mexico, injecting a good deal of local color into the hackneyed story of an insurance investigator (William Lundigan) out to find a missing colleague and a stolen jewel.

Frustrated with the films he was directing, Wise reached a point where he thought it would be better to return to editing, which allowed him to be more creative, than to continue to churn out programmers that did not rouse his imagination. However, whatever doubts he had about the course of his career were put to rest with *Blood on the Moon* [1948]. After almost five years in the B-unit, Wise rose to the top echelon at RKO with this offbeat western. The script revolves around the familiar situation of a roaming cowboy (Robert Mitchum) caught in the middle of a conflict between two rival groups. There is nothing ordinary, though, about Wise's pictorial treatment. Relying on cameraman Nicholas Musuraca's flair for chiaroscuro photography, the director molded *Blood on the Moon* in the dense film-noir style so closely associated with RKO in the '40s. The dialogue is sparse and the overall tone of the film very moody. Although rewarding western fans with some exciting action sequences, Wise clearly strove to veer away from the genre's more celebrated stereotypes. A conspicuous example of this is the gutty fist fight between Mitchum and Robert Preston. Staged with low camera angles and contrasted lighting in an oppressively low-ceilinged set, it brought a dark

The three Roberts— Mitchum, Wise and Preston— on the set of
Blood on the Moon.

brand of realism that had rarely been seen in the western before. "I thought a fight like that ought to be something that absolutely knocks you out, so I made it look like a hard, grappling kind of fight. When Mitchum finally makes it, he's really on his heels."

RKO's production chief, Dore Schary, had been instrumental in ensuring that Wise get his big leap forward with *Blood on the Moon*. When Schary submitted the screenplay of *The Set-Up* [1949] to Wise, he made yet another fundamental contribution to the director's career. Based on the long narrative poem by Joseph Moncure March, the script, written by Art Cohn, a former sportswriter with no previous screen credits, was a hard-hitting, unflinching exposé of the brutality of the boxing racket. Full of enthusiasm, Wise quickly set to work on the project with producer Richard Goldstone. No sooner had they begun when Howard Hughes purchased the always financially strapped studio and put all in-development productions on hold. Although RKO had suffered reorganizations in the past, the studio's future under Hughes' ownership seemed shaky. Schary soon quit, and Wise too decided to leave the studio he had called home for sixteen years. But first he wanted to complete this film he cared for passionately. After several weeks of uncertainty, word finally came that since *The Set-Up* was so well along into preparation, it would be the first project reactivated.

Robert Ryan, himself an undefeated inter-collegiate boxing champion while at Dartmouth, exudes inarticulate dignity as Stoker Thompson, the over-the-hill, small-time boxer who persists in an impossible pursuit of better opportunities. The film starts with Stoker having an argument with his wife (Audrey Totter), and goes on to show his preparation for a fight in the dressing room, the four-round battle with a younger opponent that he is supposed to throw, his victory, and the punishment imposed on him by the promoter who had bought off his crooked manager. One of the fascinating aspects of the film is that the story is told in real time. This experiment entailed one of several technical challenges Wise had to meet. The film opens with the camera traveling past a clock at 9:05 PM and ends with a reversal of the same shot at 10:17 PM. For the closing, Wise made several takes of the clock at different times, and when he got the film edited, used the one that was closest to the seventy-two-minute running time.

Wise directs Audrey Totter and Robert Ryan.

The Set-Up is a triumph of cinematic construction and psychological acuity. Wise's visceral evocation of a dingy milieu populated by hopeful novices, fading veterans, gamblers, sensation-hungry spectators, and racketeers reverberates with acutely observed details of character and decor. To perceptive eyes around the globe, the film heralded the consolidation of an arresting directorial talent, proving the heights to which Wise could rise when confronted with material suited to his sensibilities.

Sol C. Siegel, a leading producer at 20th Century-Fox in the late '40s and early '50s, was so impressed by *Blood on the Moon* that he invited Wise to join the studio. Wise signed a non-exclusive three-year contract with Fox and immediately began work on an original story by Edna and Edward Anhalt titled *Quarantine*. The project was temporarily shelved due to problems with the script (*Quarantine* later became Elia Kazan's *Panic in the Streets* [1950]), and independent producer Milton Sperling approached Wise about doing a woman's picture at Warner Bros. with

Eleanor Parker, Patricia Neal, and Ruth Roman. Stimulated by the prospect of directing such famous stars, as well as by the peculiar demands of a tricky genre new to him, Wise readily accepted the offer. This was not a breach of his Fox contract since, under the conditions of his agreement, he was free to pursue projects at other studios.

Wise knew he was treading potentially mawkish territory with *Three Secrets* [1950], but he believed he could imbue it with a solid dramatic sense without falling prey to its more sentimental aspects. The film centers on the relationship between three women, each of whom had given up a son for adoption years before, and now converge on a mountain resort after being convinced that it is their child who is the sole survivor of a plane crash on a nearby mountainside. Wise's seriousness was rewarded in the form of an absorbing drama that successfully weaves together the three separate stories while maintaining an air of suspense as to who the real mother is. Critics of the day lauded him for the way he substituted honesty for schmaltz and for the sense of realism he communicated, particularly in the scenes that show the mountain climbers' preparations for the rescue.

Dialogue director Anthony Jowitt, Wise, and Patricia Neal on the set of **Three Secrets**.

Wise's first film for Fox, *Two Flags West* [1950], uses a little-known proclamation by President Lincoln—which permitted prisoners of war to join the Union Army to combat Indians—as the springboard for the story of a Confederate Colonel (Joseph Cotten) who is sent to a fort commanded by an embittered Major (Jeff Chandler) whose unthinking actions cause a conflict with the Indians. Wise was unhappy with producer Casey Robinson's screenplay and tried to bow out of the assignment, but production head Darryl Zanuck persuaded him to stay on, arguing that the film would be one of the studio's top offerings for the year. Reluctantly, Wise resigned himself to the project, planning to overcome the script's basic weakness by giving it a lush visual treatment. Since it was going to be shot in Technicolor, he requested the services of cinematographer Winton C. Hoch, celebrated for his collaborations with John Ford (*Three Godfathers* [1948], *She Wore a Yellow Ribbon* [1949]). The seven-week location filming near Santa Fe, New Mexico, was about to begin when Zanuck told Wise that, under a revised budget, the film would have to be made in black and white. Hoch was strictly a Technicolor cameraman and had to be replaced at the last minute by Fox's premier director of photography, Leon Shamroy.

Together, Wise and Shamroy managed to endow the film with a brooding visual quality, exploring the rugged beauty of the New Mexico setting to its fullest. The shooting was difficult and had to be stopped on several occasions because of sand storms. Wise took advantage of the sometimes inclement weather to extract dramatically expressive shots, particularly in the scenes preceding the Indian attack on the fort. The long battle required seventy-nine different camera setups and demonstrates Wise's deftness at staging large-scale action sequences. Even Zanuck was impressed by the rushes he viewed in Hollywood while the company was on location, to the extent that he sent Wise congratulatory telegrams. In the end, however, Wise's strong visual approach could not outweigh the fundamental problems in the script.

Wise also had misgivings about another film Zanuck talked him into directing. *House on Telegraph Hill* [1951] is a suspenser along the lines of many others in which a wife, on the basis of a few pieces of evidence, concludes that her husband is trying to kill her. The story differs only in that the heroine is a Polish concentration camp inmate (Valentina Cortesa) who takes the identity of a fellow prisoner in order to emigrate to the United States, where she marries her surrogate son's guardian (Richard Basehart). Even though the grimly realistic introductory scenes at the concentration camp might suggest a character study of some consequence, they are used primarily to supply a motive for the borrowing of the deceased friend's identity, after which the film settles into a competent albeit conventional lady-in-distress mystery complete with first-person narration, Gothic sets, and atmospheric black-and-white photography.

No twisting of the arm was necessary to convince Wise to take on *The Day the Earth Stood Still* [1951], the landmark science-fiction film that became a pivotal title in the renaissance of the genre in the 1950s. Prior to this time, science fiction was largely the province of simplistic and quickly made serials that catered to the young Saturday-matinee audience. Aliens were the enemy and the action took place either in space or on another planet. Producer Julian Blaustein, writer Edmund H. North, and Wise saw science fiction in more literary terms as a means to tell a cautionary tale. In the present case, the arrival of a spaceship in Washington, D.C., carrying an emissary (Michael Rennie) who comes to Earth to exhort the nations of the world to put an end to their belligerent ways. North's refreshingly serious screenplay offered Wise that fusion of moral theme and entertainment value that is the backbone of his best works.

The Day the Earth Stood Still.

Although the film deals with a fantastic premise, Wise infused it with a feeling of realistic urgency through the use of his, by now, well-honed quasi-documentary techniques.

At a time when growing distrust presided over the relations between countries, and with the world clearly divided into two warring blocks that were arming themselves for the apocalypse, *The Day the Earth Stood Still* was a powerful voice for peaceful coexistence. And, perhaps more importantly, it presented for the first time an alien visitor as a non-aggressor, one whose mission was to deliver both a plea and an ultimatum for concord. Not surprisingly, this appeal for harmony was hardly a popular one during the Korean War, a fact reflected in the Army's refusal to provide military equipment for the production. Despite dramatic changes in the political scene since 1951, the film still retains the power of its timeless message while also offering stark observations into man's often unthinking and violent reaction to things unknown.

In 1949, Wise and Mark Robson, already anxious to be in charge of their own projects, formed a small company, Aspen Pictures. It was an uphill struggle for the independent-minded directors to secure financing, but they were able to produce two films on their own. The first, *The Captive City* [1952], directed by Wise, was inspired by the findings of the

Senate Committee investigating political corruption and organized crime that attracted a great deal of attention with its televised hearings in the early '50s, making a celebrity of Senator Estes Kefauver. Wise's film was part of a cycle of semi-documentary exposés that included titles like *The Underworld Story* [1950], *The Sellout* [1952], *The Turning Point* [1952], and *The Phenix City Story* [1955]. These films invariably depicted individuals of integrity rising above the prevailing public apathy and pitting themselves against the mighty forces of the Mob.

The disclosures of the Kefauver Committee prompted Wise to look for a story that would show the insidious encroachment of the underworld in smaller cities around the country. A series of articles by famed crime reporter Alvin Josephy, Jr., relating his own experiences as the editor of a newspaper in a Midwestern town, provided the factual framework for the taut thriller. Shooting every scene, both interior and exterior, on actual locations in Reno, Nevada, and employing a cast of unknowns (this was John Forsythe's first film lead), Wise achieved in *The Captive City* a sense of complete realism, heightened by Lee Garmes' splendid deep-focus black-and-white camera work. In this film, Garmes was the first to use the wide-angle Hoge Lens, developed over a period of eleven years by Ralph Hoge, the key grip for *Citizen Kane*'s innovative cinematographer, Gregg Toland. This fast lens reduced lighting requirements by fifty percent, greatly facilitating shooting in cramped interiors. At the same time, it also had a tremendous depth of field that allowed the foreground and background action to remain in perfect focus.

Although it was sold by the publicity department as the film that "pulls no punches about who pulls the strings in gangland's reign of terror," *The Captive City* ultimately had a greater impact on Senator Kefauver than it did on the paying public. Kefauver, in fact, not only agreed to endorse the film, but also appears in its epilogue. Despite good reviews, the film was not a commercial success, and Aspen ceased operation after its second production, the South Seas drama *Return to Paradise* [1953], directed by Robson.

Back on the Fox lot, Wise made a rare venture into comedy with *Something for the Birds* [1952], an easygoing satire culled from the political headlines of the day that took some lighthearted jibes at the Washington political scene. The story centered on a determined woman (Patricia Neal, in her third and final film with Wise) who comes to Washington to crusade for the safety of the California condor only to find her every effort blocked by special-interest lobbyists. The main purpose of the production was to provide a made-to-order vehicle for Edmund Gwenn, the congenial British character actor who had had great success as a counterfeiter in *Mister 880* [1950]. In *Something for the Birds*, Gwenn has a somewhat similar role—instead of forging one-dollar bills, he pilfers invitations to swanky Washington parties, passing himself off as a retired Admiral.

Wise and his son Robert Allen next to the Technicolor camera on location for **Destination Gobi***.*

Wise's final entries in his Fox contract were two very dissimilar World War II films. *Destination Gobi* [1953] is an anomaly in the career of a director so concerned with verisimilitude. The story follows the exploits of a team of meteorologists led by a tough Navy officer (Richard Widmark) in the Gobi Desert and their interaction with the native Mongols. Although the basis for this unusual adventure is factual—the armed forces did establish weather observation posts in the Gobi Desert and had ninety saddles flown to that distant corner as gifts for a tribe of Mongols—the accent is on action tempered with comedy, with little regard for credibility. The film, Wise's first in color, was, once again, one which he did not want to make.

In marked contrast to *Destination Gobi*'s tongue-in-cheek, almost farcical approach, *The Desert Rats* [1953] deals with men in war in the rigorously authentic style Wise favors. *The Desert Fox* [1951], a chronicle of Field Marshal Rommel's defeat in the North Africa campaign, became a box-office hit despite being accused in some quarters of showing the Nazi general in too sympathetic a light. To cash in on its success and at the same time appease the malcontents, Fox concocted *The Desert Rats* as a follow-up that shifted the focus to the allied side. *The Desert Rats* relates the valiant resistance of an Australian division against the seemingly invincible German forces. The compact eighty-eight-minute film is made memorable by several action highlights—the raid on the ammunition dump received the most praise—and by the overall quality of the acting. James Mason, who starred in *The Desert Fox*, reprised his Rommel characterization, appearing in only a few scenes, notably in a tense verbal match with Richard Burton.

An interesting appendage of Wise's concern with realism is his insistence on a homogeneity of accents in his films. In *The Desert Rats*, James Mason speaks German with his compatriots and English with a distinctive German accent in his exchange with Burton. All the other actors were either British or Australian, guaranteeing their believability in their parts. Wise never subscribed to the time-honored Hollywood practice of mixing a variety of speech patterns on the soundtrack. The stars of *Helen of Troy*, Italian Rossana Podesta and French Jack Sernas, had their voices dubbed so that they would not conflict with those of the predominantly British supporting cast. For *The Sound of Music*, a film set in Austria and about Austrians, Wise refused to cast any locals with a German accent in smaller roles. "I wanted to give the feeling that these people are speaking their own language. Since I had Julie Andrews, who is English, and Christopher Plummer, who is Canadian-English, I decided to make the film English-speaking with English accents. I had a voice coach come along and work with the children, who were all American, to give them a little English accent, just enough to make it all consistent."

His obligation with Fox fulfilled, Wise returned to Warner Bros. for another woman's picture, *So Big* [1953]. Edna Ferber's sprawling Pulitzer Prize-winning saga of motherly love and sacrifice had previously been the source of two features—in 1925, with Colleen Moore, and in 1932, with Barbara Stanwyck. Like its predecessors, Wise's version has an episodic structure, dictated by the need to compress three decades of the central character's experience into 101 minutes of film. One of the reasons he undertook the project was the chance it gave him to work with Jane Wyman. The actress turns in a beautifully modulated performance as Selina, a young woman who is left penniless by her late father and starts life anew as a teacher in a Dutch community on the outskirts of Chicago, later marrying a poor truck farmer (Sterling Hayden) and, as a widow, beating the odds to raise her son, while always maintaining a serene and understanding attitude toward her hardships. The film falters during the second half, when the focus switches to the grown son's career problems; but the first part, with its subtle and at times poignant evocation of turn-of-the-century rural life in the Midwest, displays Wise's lyrical side to touching advantage, providing a unique instance of Americana in his filmography.

Wise had first met John Houseman during the filming of *Citizen Kane*, in which Houseman served as an uncredited script consultant. Following the war, Houseman became a producer, later moving to the MGM lot, where he achieved immediate success with two all-star dramas, *The Bad and the Beautiful* [1952] and *Julius Caesar* [1953]. For his production of *Executive Suite* [1954], Cameron Hawley's best-seller of corporate business succession and politics, Houseman again assembled an impressive line-up of stars—William Holden, June Allyson, Barbara Stanwyck, Fredric March, Walter Pidgeon, Paul Douglas, Shelley Winters, Louis Calhern,

Dean Jagger, and Nina Foch. Coordinating the schedules of such a prestigious company of actors was almost as difficult for Houseman as trying to convince the studio brass that he wanted to hire an outside director. After weeks of providing sound reasons for rejecting MGM's contract directors, he was finally able to sign his sole choice, Robert Wise. The screenplay was written by Ernest Lehman (the first in his momentous association with Wise) and details the struggle for power in a modern corporation following the unexpected death of its president. The script is made up entirely of conversation scenes involving the main characters and culminates in a climactic boardroom meeting where they all gather to elect the new president.

Given the strong emphasis on dialogue, Houseman knew that only a director with Wise's editing skills would manage to give the verbose script the kind of pace that would keep it alive and full of tension. His choice proved an inspired one. Wise establishes a dynamic drive from the striking first shots—with the subjective camera acting as the dying president—and never lets up. To maintain the unflagging rhythm, Wise boldly opted to do away with fades and dissolves. "At one point, when preparing for the film," Wise reveals, "I decided I wouldn't have to use them. Because of the way the story built from the beginning and how it went along—all the people involved, all the different scenes—I thought I could keep the momentum without having to do time lapses. It seemed to me that we were so locked into dissolves and fade-outs that it became almost a cliché. There were just two or three places in *Executive Suite* where it wouldn't work; but my concept was to do the whole film with straight cuts, even when changing locales."

Producer John Houseman, Nina Foch, and Walter Pidgeon.

Wise's most prestigious film to date, *Executive Suite* was released by MGM with the fanfare befitting a production designed to celebrate the studio's thirty years in business. The critics were unanimous in their praise of the acting, writing, and directing, and the audiences came in large numbers. But this was the time when the Hollywood studios were faced with declining film attendance and dwindling box-office receipts. In response to the broadening penetration of television, a number of widescreen processes were introduced to lure the deserting patrons back. Spurred by the smashing success of the first CinemaScope feature, the Biblical epic *The Robe* [1953], each of the major studios launched massive historical spectacles that gave viewers bigger-than-life thrills that could not be replicated in the coziness of one's living room. Pleased with Wise's previous efforts for his studio, Jack Warner invited him to direct *Helen of Troy* [1955], which was to be filmed in Italy utilizing frozen funds the studio had in that European country.

From pre-production to final editing, *Helen of Troy* engaged Wise for a full year. The drawn-out filming was besieged by problems, many of them related to the fact that there was no producer assigned to the film. Although Wise would be responsible for most of the producer's duties, Jack Warner refused to give him credit, telling Wise that the executive in charge of the studio's activities in Europe would help him with the overall production aspects but was not to consider himself the producer either. The confusion about who retained control did not make the already rigorous shooting any easier for Wise. Unbeknownst to the director, the European executive sent cables to Warner contesting his every decision, and Wise was often awakened in the wee hours by calls from Hollywood asking for explanations.

Among the other problems that plagued the production was the unsatisfactory work done by the second unit. Wise always preferred to do all of his second unit himself, but, given the sheer size of *Helen of Troy*, he was forced to delegate this task to a specialist, Yakima Canutt, whose footage proved unacceptable. He was replaced by Raoul Walsh, who took over as a favor to Jack Warner, with the understanding that he would not receive credit. Wise's predicaments were not over once he wrapped shooting. Back in Hollywood, Jack Warner tampered with Wise's cut of the film. A fight between the two followed, after which the director's version was reinstated. *Helen of Troy* was another of Wise's excursions into untried territory; the unfulfilling experience precluded any future return to epics.

Despite their disagreements, Warner wanted Wise to remain at the studio. But by the time *Helen of Troy* was released, MGM, impressed with the excellent reviews and strong box-office amassed by *Executive Suite*, offered Wise a lucrative three-year contract. His first film under the new agreement was *Tribute to a Bad Man* [1956], a western that deals with a self-reliant horse breeder who dispenses his own brand of justice within his vast domains. As he had done before with *Blood on the Moon* and *Two Flags West*, Wise took a strong visual approach to the genre. Shot in color and CinemaScope against the dazzling backdrop of the Colorado Rockies, the film's chief asset is its great pictorial beauty. Originally,

Spencer Tracy was going to play the title role, but after a few days' shooting in the high-altitude location, he asked to be replaced. James Cagney stepped in and brought his trademark vitality and intensity to the part. Despite the film's accomplishment as a character study and a detailed evocation of frontier life in the late 1800s, Wise decided not to make any more westerns after *Tribute to a Bad Man*: "I found out I really didn't enjoy making them. They're big and cumbersome; you're always at the mercy of the weather; and horses don't take direction very well. Also, by that time, I felt that the western genre seemed overdone."

The high point of Wise's stay at MGM, *Somebody Up There Likes Me* [1956], was based on the autobiography of boxing great Rocky Graziano. By temperament, Wise would not be inclined to tackle a script that resembled something he had done previously, and Graziano's story attracted him exactly for the dissimilarities to his earlier boxing film, *The Set-Up*. The protagonist is not a failed veteran clinging to one last chance to prove himself, but a pugnacious juvenile who parlays his hostile behavior into a career in the rings, eventually winning the title of world champ. The fight game is seen not as a brutal racket but as a path toward his redemp-

Somebody Up There Likes Me: *Eileen Heckart, Wise, and Paul Newman.*

tion, in which he is immeasurably helped by his loving wife (Pier Angeli) and understanding manager (Everett Sloane). The underlying value Wise found in Ernest Lehman's screenplay was that "no matter where you're born or how tough it is, it is possible to overcome the environment and make something of yourself." Energized by Paul Newman's virtuoso, star-making performance, *Somebody Up There Likes Me* brims with vigor and physicality. Once in a while, Wise relaxes the rhythm for a few tender moments in which he brings home the theme of transcendence through love and friendship that gives the film its resonance.

Wise's two releases for 1957 both starred Jean Simmons. *This Could Be the Night* features Simmons as a public schoolteacher who takes a part-time job as a secretary in a nightclub owned by a gruff but good-hearted ex-bootlegger (Paul Douglas), where she affects the lives of co-workers and regulars alike. The producer of this charming fish-out-of-water comedy was Joe Pasternak, a specialist in Technicolor escapist musicals. Having Wise behind the camera, however, dictated that the film receive a much more realistic tone than was customary in the producer's canon. Wise persuaded Pasternak to let him shoot the film in black and white, pointing out that it would be more in keeping with the nightclub setting and the characters in the story. As for the several musical numbers inter-

spersed through the film, they are presented primarily as background action while Wise concentrates on the cleverly devised progression of Isobel Lennart's witty screenplay. There was only one area wherein Wise had to acquiesce to Pasternak's wish: "Isobel and I hated the title *This Could Be the Night*, but Joe loved it, and he already had a title-song written for it. We thought it was a very innocuous title that didn't spell out our picture at all, but we couldn't get him to change it."

In the early '50s, Aspen Pictures acquired the rights to two stories

Until They Sail*: Wise, writer Robert Anderson, and producer Charles Schnee.*

from the James Michener bestseller *Return to Paradise*. Only one was made into a film by the company: *Return to Paradise*, starring Gary Cooper. Wise was scheduled to direct the other, *Until They Sail*, but Aspen folded before he could make it. The story was then sold to Hecht-Lancaster and announced in 1954 as a forthcoming picture to be directed by Burt Lancaster. That project didn't materialize either. In 1955, the property found its way to MGM. Producer Charles Schnee wanted to reteam with Wise after *Somebody Up There Likes Me* and suggested that they film Michener's tale of four New Zealand sisters (Jean Simmons, Joan Fontaine, Piper Laurie, and Sandra Dee) and their involvement with men in uniform during World War II. Wise had hoped to shoot *Until They Sail* on location and in color, but studio economics dictated that Christchurch and Wellington be duplicated on the MGM backlot and the film made in black and white and CinemaScope. Robert Anderson's screenplay deftly weaves the interlaced stories, and Wise's understated direction keeps its lachrymose ingredients to a minimum, stressing honesty over sentimentality, particularly in the adult relationship between the characters played by Simmons and Paul Newman. *Until They Sail* was Wise's last film under long-term contract to a studio.

Wise once remarked that the most powerful method of portraying human emotions on the screen was to have the crucial moments of a film take place in a compact space. "When a clash occurs between humans confined in such a manner," he explained, "the intensification of emotion is terrific." With *Run Silent, Run Deep* [1958], he fully demonstrated his theory. Wise had art director Edward Carrere build the sets in which this suspenseful submarine drama takes place to the exact size of the real submarine he visited during research. The cramped sets allowed little

*Wise in the cramped submarine set he had built for **Run Silent, Run Deep**.*

room for the camera to maneuver, forcing Wise to convey a very real sense of closeness and claustrophobia, accentuating the antagonism between the characters forcefully portrayed by Clark Gable and Burt Lancaster. The film was produced by Lancaster's company and followed a pattern of teaming the star with another male actor of comparable stature, a formula that reaped healthy box-office in films like *Vera Cruz* [1954] (with Gary Cooper), *Gunfight at the OK Corral* [1957] (with Kirk Douglas), and *Trapeze* [1956] (with Tony Curtis). In *Run Silent, Run Deep* Lancaster plays a Lieutenant whose anticipated promotion to Captain of a submarine is thwarted when Gable is appointed to command the ship. The animosity between them escalates because of Gable's obstinate pursuit of the Japanese ship that sunk his previous commission. This highly polished film belies the fact that Wise was working from a screenplay that was continually rewritten all through shooting.

Before Wise got involved with *Run Silent, Run Deep*, independent producer Walter Wanger had contacted him about doing a film on Barbara Graham, the party-girl sent to the gas chamber for the killing of an elderly woman. The idea of using Graham's ordeal in the death row to make a strong plea against capital punishment appealed to Wise, but he felt that the first-draft screenplay written by Don Mankiewicz was intractable and dropped out of the project. When he finished his submarine thriller, Wise resumed talks with Wanger, and a new writer, Nelson Gidding, was hired. Together, Wise and Gidding shaped reporter Ed Montgomery's account of Graham's trial and execution into an incisive screenplay, and the felicitous result of their joint effort kicked off a collaboration that extended to several other projects.

Featuring Susan Hayward's powerhouse performance in the leading role, *I Want to Live!* emerged as one of the most talked-about films of 1958, giving credence to Wise's belief that such a controversial subject, if handled in a candid yet tasteful manner, could reach a large public. Wise's intention was to cause a reflection on the death penalty by casting an unblinking eye on the psychological horror of a prisoner awaiting her death. The film stands as a notable example of his technique of making a powerful statement strictly through the telling of the story, without resorting to sermonizing.

I Want to Live!: *Wise and Susan Hayward.*

Still, the film raised heated criticism in some quarters for allegedly portraying Graham as a woman unjustly condemned for murder. "We've been accused, particularly by law-enforcement people, of saying that an innocent woman went to the gas chamber. This is not true. She was not innocent; she was found guilty. I suppose there's a certain amount of sympathy that goes to her because of the nature of the film and the fact that Susan is playing her, but we never literally say she's innocent."

When he completed *I Want to Live!*, Wise knew that it would do more for his career than any film he had directed before. Come Oscar time, Susan Hayward received a Best Actress award. Among the film's five other nominations was one for Wise, his first in the Best Director category. The film's accolades and potent box-office gave Wise the impetus to seek greater control over his work. In a few of his past films, notably *Mystery in Mexico* and *Helen of Troy*, Wise had unofficially acted as the producer. On his next film, Wise was billed as producer-director, and shortly thereafter he formed his own production company (first known as B&P, and then as Argyle) and began negotiating his deals with the studios on a film-per-film basis.

Odds Against Tomorrow [1959], a bank-robbery yarn laced with a puissant anti-racist allegory, was a watershed in Wise's career in more ways than just being his initial producing credit. It was his last black-and-white film shot in the standard aspect ratio and the culmination of the grittily realistic style with which he had become so closely identified since the late '40s. Sadly, Wise was never to return to this type of film because the changing face of the industry all but extinguished small-scale, black-and-white productions. Obviously unaware of this impending development, Wise offered a keenly perceptive encapsulation of his stylistic intentions in the non-anamorphic films he had made after the introduction of the widescreen processes when he told an interviewer in the late '50s: "Recently I've been fortunate to be able to make a number of pictures in the 1:85 frame, black and white, where I had much more opportunity to think in terms of film, montage, and sound. What I'm trying to do is use film in its complete sense—visual, sound, music—in as exciting, interesting, dramatic, offbeat and effective a manner as I can. I don't mean that everything I'm doing is new; much of it had been established years ago but had become lost with the advent of the enlarged size of the frame."

The main characters in *Odds Against Tomorrow* are not professional thieves but partners of chance who see a bank robbery as a way out of their individual predicaments. The theft is minutely planned by a former police officer (Ed Begley) who enlists the aid of a black singer (Harry Belafonte) and a bigoted Southerner (Robert Ryan). But the enmity between the latter two scuttles the enterprise. When Wise accepted Harry Belafonte's offer to direct the film (the first film made by Belafonte's company, Harbel), another drama about a black-and-white hate relationship, *The Defiant Ones* [1958], was enjoying a successful run in theaters.

In the Stanley Kramer film, the black and the white overcome their prejudices and accept one another at the end. Wise found a similar denouement in the original novel by William McGivern and the first-draft screenplay for *Odds Against Tomorrow*, but felt that his movie should not have the same resolution. He proposed that the other side of the coin be shown: that hate destroys. At the film's end, Ryan and Belafonte furiously try to kill each other, and both perish in an explosion. In an ironic twist, the police cannot determine which body is which. Instead of saying that in the ideal world blacks and whites will get along, Wise suggests that the less they get along, the more they destroy each other. In spite of its dramatic punch, Wise believes that audiences of the day were put off by the nihilistic ending. "Maybe we failed in working our characters up to the point where we could destroy them in high tragedy terms that would make people feel it deeply and think about the whole picture."

Despite its disappointing performance at the box-office, *Odds Against Tomorrow* received outstanding reviews and is widely regarded as one of Wise's chefs-d'oeuvre. Among its staunch admirers was Jean-Pierre Melville, France's premier film-noir director and a particular aficionado of Wise's work in that genre, who admitted to having watched it more than a hundred times. The two directors met in Paris in 1971. "Melville took me into a projection room to show me a sequence from one of his pictures in which he had used the sound effect of a door closing out of *Odds Against Tomorrow*. He said, 'That was in your picture,' and seemed so pleased with that. He was a tremendous fan of the film."

Wise's next film, also set in New York City and throwing into relief the same moral that hate destroys, met with extraordinary critical and popular reception, opening a new phase in his career. The only major genre manifestly absent in Wise's filmography at this time was the musical. He rectified this omission with the stunning *West Side Story* [1961]. The landmark Broadway show from which it derived was conceived by choreographer/director Jerome Robbins as a modern-day retelling of the Romeo and Juliet story with the star-crossed lovers caught in the middle of a conflict between rival street gangs fighting for the same turf. United Artists had entrusted the Mirisch Company with making the film, and they in turn selected Wise to be in charge of the six-million-dollar project. The choice of a director who had never done a musical before seems most apt in the case of *West Side Story*, which is closer in tone to the rugged, socially aware films Wise excelled in. "They thought," Wise says, "that maybe somebody who had done highly dramatic films that dug into people and conflicts of all kinds might be better at doing this particular musical than anybody else." Besides, Wise was familiar with all the technical aspects of making musicals. Back in the '30s, he had worked on several of the Fred Astaire/Ginger Rogers films at RKO, first as a sound effects and music editor and then as an assistant editor.

Wise poses with Fred Astaire after receiving his Oscars for producing and co-directing **West Side Story**.

Wise faced numerous challenges in his first roadshow film. Chief among them was the fact that Robbins would be his co-director. The tandem arrangement was, of course, completely new to Wise, and months went by before the two could reach an agreement on what their modus operandi would be. An entire year was spent in pre-production—Ernest Lehman wrote the adaptation, associate producer Saul Chaplin organized a whole musical department, Robbins and Wise interviewed hundreds of candidates for the parts, and Robbins and his assistants rehearsed the dancers extensively. From its inception, the filmmakers decided that *West Side Story* would be unlike any other film musical, one in which all the elements of film grammar would mesh to turn this blend of drama, music, and dance into a one-of-a-kind moviegoing experience. The cinematic style they strove for had to combine the realistic requirements of the film medium with the more stylized conventions of the theatrical presentation. So important was the creation of a unique visual presentation that virtually every major Hollywood cameraman was considered, and many of them tested, until Wise settled on Daniel L. Fapp as the one who would break with convention and go for the rather radical approach he had in mind.

After six months of shooting and seven months of post-production, *West Side Story* emerged as a singular film, one that revolutionized the screen musical. Prior to *West Side Story*, musical and dance numbers were usually shot in long takes with the camera mounted on a crane; very few or no cuts interrupted the fluidity of the camera moves. Always the realist, Wise felt uncomfortable with characters that break into song and dance halfway through sentences. In attempting to put the audience in a frame of mind to accept tough street kids singing and dancing, Wise drew upon his trademark staccato cutting and employed editing as an extension of the music and the dancing. The resultant vigor and

Wise is presented to Queen Elizabeth at the Command Performance of **West Side Story** *in London.*

energy electrified viewers the world over. "Taking from the original to the final film, I think *West Side Story* was more of a challenge, more of a creative accomplishment than any of my films," says Wise. His two years of hard work were rewarded with a hefty box-office take and an abundance of awards, including ten Oscars: best film, direction, supporting actor (George Chakiris), supporting actress (Rita Moreno), cinematography, art direction, editing, costume design, musical adaptation, and sound.

"I have no problems going from a big project to a small one," Wise confesses. "If the story happens to catch me right at the time, I want to do it." Wise's follow-up to the massive *West Side Story* were two smaller films, his last black-and-white efforts, both shot in the Panavision widescreen process. Once again having New York City as a backdrop, *Two for the Seesaw* [1962] is the film version of William Gibson's bittersweet, opposites-attract, two-character play. Robert Mitchum is Jerry Ryan, a lawyer from Omaha, recently separated from his wife, who moves to New York and gets romantically involved with free-wheeling Gittel Mosca, played by Shirley MacLaine. On the Broadway stage, the roles were essayed by Henry Fonda and Anne Bancroft. When the film was released, many reviewers chided Wise for having bypassed the original couple in favor of bigger film stars. However, Wise had no voice in the casting of the leads—they had already been signed when he was offered the project. Wise himself had doubts about their suitability before filming began, but once they started working together, he was very pleased with the special quality they brought to their parts. With the notable exception of *West Side Story* and *The Sound of Music*, *Two for the Seesaw* is Wise's only adaptation of a stage play. In his persuasive mise en scène, he avoided opening the theatrical show up too much, incorporating one of its important elements, the set with the two apartments side by side, without sacrificing the smooth narrative flow.

Instigated by a favorable review of Shirley Jackson's disturbing ghost story *The Haunting of Hill House*, Wise purchased a copy of the book and set about reading it at the Goldwyn Studios, where he was preparing *West Side Story*. As he recalls: "I was reading one of the very scary passages—hackles were going up and down my neck—when Nelson Gidding, who was working in the office next door to mine, burst through the door to ask me a question. I literally jumped about three feet out of my chair. I said, 'If it can do that to me sitting and reading, it ought to be something I want to make a picture out of.'" Gidding wrote the screenplay and Wise tried to activate the project when he finished *West Side Story*, but the Mirisch company had lost interest in it. MGM picked up the project and *The Haunting* was released in 1963. It was a commercial failure, but slowly began to attract a following and is regarded today as one of the key titles in the haunted-house genre.

The story's setting is Hill House, a New England mansion with a history of macabre happenings. A group of psychic researchers gather to study the place, and one of its members, Eleanor, played by Julie Harris, falls prey to its spell. *The Haunting* stresses the psychological aspect of the story, maintaining a basic ambiguity as to how much is real and how much is a product of Eleanor's imagination. In his first chiller since his beginnings as a director under Val Lewton's tutelage, Wise applies his old mentor's theory that if seen things are scary, unseen things are scarier, and extracts truly frightening moments by merely implying terror through the inspired use of sound and the dense black-and-white photography. Wise believes that a director "can go farther in terms of style in stories of the supernatural. A film like *The Haunting* is a lot of fun to make because you can do so much with offbeat photography and the use of sound and music. Val always said that the greatest fear that people have is the fear of the unknown. Unlike so many films that are made now which try to scare by showing the most monstrous things you can possibly think, *The Haunting* frightens the viewer by just suggesting them."

Another book the Mirisch Company acquired for Wise was *The Sand Pebbles*, Richard MacKenna's voluminous account of conflicts in the strife-torn China of 1926. Playwright Robert Anderson was already working on the screenplay when United Artists, concerned with the size and cost of the production, put it in turnaround. Bent upon making the film, Wise pitched the project to Darryl Zanuck. The mogul shared Wise's enthusiasm and authorized the purchase of the film rights by 20th Century-Fox. Realizing that paring the novel down into a shooting screenplay and finding the best locations (the Chinese government would not allow an American film to be made there at the time) would take at least an entire year, Wise began to look for something to do in the interim and ended up accepting Fox's offer to produce and direct a film version of Rodgers and Hammerstein's *The Sound of Music*. Wise was unfamiliar with the show, but Ernest Lehman's screenplay together with Saul Chaplin's assurance that it would make for a first-rate musical were enough to convince him that the romanticized story of the von Trapp family was worth his while.

Wise and Boris Leven.

Curiously, the film Wise took on to fill in the waiting period became the most spectacular success of his career. He wrote to Robert Anderson prior to shooting: "If we can fight off too much sentimentality and the syrup that is inherent in the basic material and give it an exciting cinematic treatment, perhaps we can make it a much better picture than it was a play. What am I talking about, the picture should only be as successful!" Wise's version of *The Sound of Music* [1965] far exceeded his preliminary expectations and went on to become one of the best-loved films of all time. Many factors should be mentioned when discussing its colossal success—the beauty of the songs, the breathtaking Austrian scenery, Julie Andrews' performance, the handsomeness of the overall presentation—but it all boils down to Wise's shrewdness in surrounding himself with a choice group of collaborators and his artistry in transposing the stage show in such a highly imaginative way. Backed by the quintessential Wise crew—production designer Boris Leven, cinematographer Ted McCord, editor William Reynolds, production illustrator Maurice Zuberano—the director made an exhilarating fairy tale of a musical that is at all times consistent with his feelings about human dignity and freedom of spirit. In addition to record-breaking box-office, *The Sound of Music* received ten Academy Award nominations, winning in the best picture, director, editing, sound, and musical adaptation categories.

The Sand Pebbles [1966] is perhaps Wise's most personal film, an intensely moving, multi-layered outcry against war and intolerance that used an event of the recent past to shed light on a decidedly current issue. "I thought it was time," Wise says, "that the American public was reminded that the phrase 'Yankees Go Home!,' which was very prominent in World War II, was not born then, but had been going on in a lot of areas around this world all through the century. Our gunboats on the Yangtze River in the 1920s were a symbol of that. I thought the film had elements of warning to us about what we were doing in Vietnam; that this was not the way to go in the Far East, having our troops there in battle with the local people."

The location filming in Taiwan and Hong Kong proved to be the longest and most arduous of Wise's career, as it was beset by labor disputes, language barriers, unpredictable tides, and, above all, terrible weather conditions. These contretemps helped swell the film's cost to $12 million, but having such a whopping hit as *The Sound of Music* under his belt, Wise was given carte blanche by the Fox executives to make his thought-provoking, eye-filling magnum opus as he saw fit. *The Sand Pebbles* is a vast and panoramic tale, but Wise never loses sight of the human interest that is the raison d'être of this epic with a soul. The title refers to the way the Chinese allude to the crew of the gunboat U.S.S. *San Pablo*, mobilized for patrol in the waters of the Yangtze River at a time when the surging Nationalist movement tried to force foreign powers out of the

STAR!: *Producer Saul Chaplin, Julie Andrews, Wise, and choreographer Michael Kidd.*

country. *The Sand Pebbles* is admirable for its sympathetic view of all sides of the intricate political situation it portrays. Rather than taking sides, Wise opts for a grave meditation on man's inhumanity to man and the pressing need for understanding among the nations of the world.

Wise had no plans of giving his future up to blockbuster musicals, but he enjoyed working with Julie Andrews so much that he requested that his company produce the second film in her two-picture deal with Fox. The reteaming of Wise and Andrews stirred tremendous interest in the industry; Fox allocated $14 million for *STAR!* [1968], a lavish recreation of incidents in the life of stage celebrity Gertrude Lawrence. The project was developed from scratch as a tailor-made vehicle for Andrews. While Wise was away in the Orient, Saul Chaplin, Wise's associate producer and right-hand man on *West Side Story* and *The Sound of Music*, oversaw the writing of the original script and the pre-production planning. Once Wise put the finishing touches on *The Sand Pebbles*, he took the helm of his third consecutive roadshow film. Shooting required 149 days, divided between the Hollywood studios, where 185 sets were built, and locations in New York, London, and southern France. Immune to the rigors of hard work (he toiled a total of fifty-five months straight on the Fox roadshows), Wise spent a few more months in post-production before the three-hour-long *STAR!* was unveiled to the public.

After previews that generated enthusiastic reactions from the audience, the film went into limited release and fared poorly at the box-office. In a desperate attempt to recoup its investment, Fox had the film cut to two hours and re-released under the title of *Those Were the Happy Days*, but it too failed. Apart from sporadic TV airings of the shortened print, *Star!* remained largely unseen for twenty-five years. In 1993, with the first showings of the full-length version on cable TV and its subsequent release on home video, it finally reached a large and appreciative audience. Wise's opulent ode to a bygone era of theater and music hall entertainment had at last been rescued from oblivion.

Wise was still in pre-production for *STAR!* when he announced that, regardless of the story, his next project would be very contemporary. In his last three films, he had to delve into different periods of the first half of the twentieth century and meticulously reproduce them for the cameras. Now he longed to return to a modern setting and hopefully address some major issue of the day. The answer to his wishes came in the form of Michael Crichton's *The Andromeda Strain*. Simulating an official top-secret document, the book described the efforts of four scientists racing against the clock to isolate and control a lethal microorganism brought back to Earth by a space probe. Wise scrupulously duplicated this feeling of factuality in his film. *The Andromeda Strain* [1971] was made on a generous budget, but Wise refused to cast any big stars for fear that their visibility could hamper his non-fictional approach. The real stars of the film are Boris Leven's ingenious sets for the underground laboratory where most of the action takes place. One of them, representing the core of the facility, was seventy feet high, and, in order to accommodate it, Universal Studio's largest stage had to be excavated seventeen feet into the ground. The core is the setting for the last ten minutes of the film, an edge-of-your-seat conclusion to a suspenseful science-fact thriller made up of count-less little pieces assembled by Wise with the precision of a watchmaker.

The Hindenburg: Wise with continuity illustrator Tom Wright.

In 1971, twenty years after their first foray into independent production, Wise and Mark Robson decided to have another go at it. They formed the Filmakers Group and installed themselves at the Columbia Studios. There, Robson directed *Happy Birthday, Wanda June* [1971] and *Limbo* [1972], and Wise developed *Two People*, the story of a deserter from the Vietnam War who meets and falls in love with a fashion model on his way back to the United States after three years in exile. Wise and Columbia were at loggerheads over the casting of the female lead. The studio wanted a name actress, the director an unknown. After much testing, Wise picked newcomer Lindsay Wagner for the role, but Columbia refused to go ahead with the film. Wise then moved the project and the Filmakers Group to the Universal lot. In a radical departure from the expensive movies of late, and especially from the claustrophobic atmosphere of *The Andromeda Strain, Two People* [1973] was made on a modest budget and shot entirely on locations in Morocco, Paris, and New York. In spite of its topicality, the romantic drama received very limited release and is possibly Wise's least-seen film. "I don't think I ever had a bigger disappointment in terms of reviews and audience reaction. At the time, I thought it was a good love story with an important theme, but nobody seemed to care for it."

Wise's mastery of the technical aspects of filmmaking was once again put to test when he undertook the grandiose task of dramatizing the ill-fated last voyage of the dirigible *Hindenburg* in May of 1937. Universal had been trying to get a film made on the subject for some time, but their attempts usually stumbled on the basic question of how to turn the real-life tragedy into a compelling narrative. The cause for the ship's much publicized explosion at its arrival in Lakehurst was never found, and for many years speculations abounded. The premise of *The Hindenburg* [1975] is that the catastrophe resulted from an act of sabotage perpetrated by a crew member disgruntled with the Nazi regime. George C. Scott stars as a Luftwaffe officer sent by Dr. Goebbels to investigate the people aboard the ship and quell any attempts at destroying her. Once he had a screenplay with a solid dramatic handle, Wise concentrated on how to physically resurrect the *Hindenburg*. With the help of some of Hollywood's finest technicians, the dirigible came alive as a composite of a twenty-seven-foot model, matte paintings, and full-size recreations of some of its sections. The illusion was so perfect that the film received special Academy Awards for visual effects and sound editing.

Again, a small project followed a large one. *Audrey Rose* (1977), written by Frank De Felitta, based on his own best-selling novel, had only four major characters and treated the difficult issue of reincarnation in a sober, austere fashion that was quite different than such popular 1970s horror films as *The Exorcist* (1973) and *The Omen* (1976). True to the precepts that governed his entire career, Wise avoided gratuitous shock effects and concentrated on giving dramatic cogency to the story of a

*Wise with son, Rob, and grandchildren Jennifer and Patrick on the set of **Star Trek—The Motion Picture**.*

couple (John Beck and Marsha Mason) tormented by a stranger (Anthony Hopkins) who claims that their young daughter (Susan Swift) is the re-incarnation of his own daughter Audrey Rose. This intense chamber film is highlighted by emotionally charged confrontations among the leading characters, which culminate in a disturbing scene of regression that attests to Wise's particular gift for extracting credible performances from child actors, a talent that he had demonstrated previously in *The Curse of the Cat People, House on Telegraph Hill, The Day the Earth Stood Still,* and *The Sound of Music.*

Part of what makes Wise's films such models of craftsmanship is the thorough mapping out of every sequence before the cameras start rolling: "I generally have my sequences storyboarded with the angles I want to shoot them in, but I always allow room to move away from aspects of that blocking if something comes up in rehearsal that works better than

I had planned. But at least I go in knowing how the scenes should progress in terms of physical action." This kind of preparation is vital on films that require extensive use of special effects.

Working with the production designer, storyboard artist and effects technicians from the earliest stages, Wise was able to successfully complete films as complex as *The Andromeda Strain* and *The Hindenburg* on time and on budget. *Star Trek—The Motion Picture* [1979], Wise's first venture into intergalactic science fiction, was to depend on special effects on a scale larger than anything he had done before. Nonetheless, Wise was not allowed enough time to plan ahead, as the film was rushed into production with an incomplete script and special effects still to be conceptualized. Considering all the problems he had to cope with, only a filmmaker of Wise's experience and skill could have turned this first theatrical feature based on the cult TV series into the visually and aurally ravishing film it became.

Ten years separate *Star Trek—The Motion Picture* from Wise's next film, the youth-oriented *Rooftops* [1989]. This long hiatus from filmmaking was marked by a series of aborted projects. Two of them, in particular, involved Wise for long periods of time: a love story set in Shanghai in the late 1940s that he had hoped to film on location, and the film version of *Zorba, the Musical*. Wise's only screen credit during that period was as executive producer of *Wisdom* [1986], in which he served as an advisor to debuting director Emilio Estevez. Besides the unrealized projects, Wise kept himself busy with other activities. He was President of the Academy of Motion Pictures Arts & Sciences for three one-year terms, and served as chairman of the Directors Guild of America's Special Projects Committee and as a trustee and chairman of the American Film Institute's Center for Advanced Film Studies. In the latter capacity, Wise spent several years working as a tutor to film students.

This contact with young people made it easy for Wise to take charge of *Rooftops*, the first production of director Taylor Hackford's independent company, New Visions. The medium-sized film returned Wise to the scene of some of his greatest triumphs, the urban landscape of New York City, more specifically the rough streets of Manhattan's Alphabet City, where a group of youths live on the rooftops of abandoned buildings and fight against a vicious drug dealer. The film mixes elements of social realism, action, and romance; although it includes some choreographed dances, it is not a musical. *Rooftops* proved that, at seventy-four, Wise was still a filmmaker in full command of his craft. The carefully composed images, the tight editing, the unflagging pace were everywhere in evidence, making one wish that Wise had not stayed away from the camera for so long.

EDITOR

Films as Editor

1939   *FIFTH AVENUE GIRL*, with William Hamilton (directed by Gregory La Cava).

       THE HUNCHBACK OF NOTRE DAME, with William Hamilton (directed by William Dieterle).

       BACHELOR MOTHER, with Henry Berman (directed by Garson Kanin).

1940   *DANCE, GIRL, DANCE* (directed by Dorothy Arzner).

       MY FAVORITE WIFE (directed by Garson Kanin).

1941   *CITIZEN KANE* (directed by Orson Welles).

       ALL THAT MONEY CAN BUY (directed by William Dieterle).

1942   *THE MAGNIFICENT AMBERSONS* (directed by Orson Welles).

       SEVEN DAYS' LEAVE (directed by Tim Whelan).

1943   *BOMBARDIER* (directed by Richard Wallace).

       THE FALLEN SPARROW (directed by Richard Wallace).

       THE IRON MAJOR (directed by Ray Enright).

Among Wise's uncredited work as an assistant to William Hamilton:

1936   *WINTERSET* (directed by Alfred Santell).

1937   *STAGE DOOR* (directed by Gregory La Cava).

       SHALL WE DANCE (directed by Mark Sandrich).

1938   *CAREFREE* (directed by Mark Sandrich).

       HAVING WONDERFUL TIME (directed by Alfred Santell and, uncredited, George Stevens).

1939   *THE STORY OF VERNON AND IRENE CASTLE* (directed by H. C. Potter).

RW:

" RKO was a small, compact studio, not so much of a factory as some of the other film companies. A lot of important talents of the '30s and '40s were working there. During my years as an assistant editor and, later, as an editor, I came in contact with several of them. Gregory La Cava was a very interesting director. He never covered very much. His pictures were very simple to put together—very few cuts, very few closeups. We didn't have a complete script on *Stage Door* until the day after we finished shooting. He would just feed it out as he was shooting. He had his script down in the bottom drawer of his desk, and the actors rarely got it until the morning they were shooting the scene. And he obviously had

Gregory La Cava and Katharine Hepburn on the set of **Stage Door**.

several versions in his desk, which he worked on before he came on the set. Actors told us that sometimes they'd come up and start trying a certain scene that wouldn't be right, and he would say, 'Wait a minute,' go to his office and, after a while, come back with a different version of it. That was the only experience I had with a director who did it day by day, piece by piece. It wasn't improvising; he had the scenes written, but they were kept for the last minute.

"Garson Kanin was completely different. He came to Hollywood from the Broadway stage and always asked for an editor on the set to help him with the coverage and the angles. When he came to do *My Favorite Wife*, I stayed with him on the set making sure that all the technical parts were right, while Mark Robson was doing the first cutting, as I had done with Billy Hamilton before. I spent a lot of time with Gar. He was not married, and, very often, we would go to the restaurant after work, have dinner together, a few drinks, and talk about things. It was a very close, warm relationship.

"William Dieterle had a habit of directing with white gloves on, the kind of cotton gloves film editors used to wear in the old days. Everybody had a feeling that was because of

Walter Huston, James Craig and William Dieterle (with obligatory white gloves) during the filming of **All That Money Can Buy**.

some germ or dirt phobia. I showed that to be false one day when I was on the set of *All that Money Can Buy* out in the RKO ranch. He was shooting a street scene in the village and the street was full of mud. They were ready to start shooting when he noticed that somehow there wasn't any mud on a certain part of a carriage wheel. He quickly pulled off the glove, got his hand in that mud, got some of it, rubbed it on the wheel and got it set just right for the camera. Then he wiped his hand on his pants, put the glove back on, and continued working. That glove thing was simply superstition. He believed in readings of the stars and astrology. In fact, a couple of weeks before he started to shoot on *The Hunchback of Notre Dame*, Billy Hamilton and I got a few odd shots in the dailies, completely out of the blue. One was of a soldier on horseback with a spear, another was of a trumpeter up against the sky. We didn't know what they were until we found out later that Dieterle's wife, herself a confirmed astrologer, had predicted that he should start shooting on a certain date. So he went out deliberately and started the picture by making those few shots.

"I didn't know what I was getting into when I first came on *Citizen Kane*, but, when I started seeing the dailies coming in, I knew it was something quite special. However, I don't think any of us anticipated that it would come down through

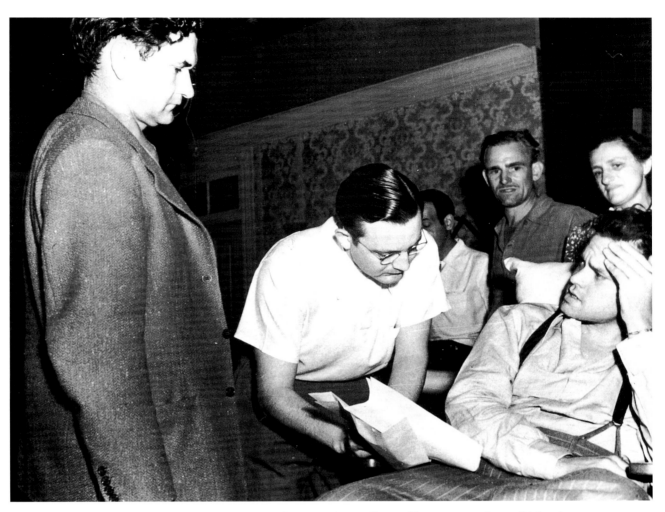

Between takes on **Citizen Kane**: *assistant director Ed Donahue, Wise, Orson Welles, and script supervisor Mollie Kent.*

the years being considered by film buffs and critics the best film ever made. I venture to say—my own personal opinion—that the only film Orson ever made that he had complete concentration on was *Citizen Kane*. That was his big opportunity and nothing else seemed to exist in his life. *The Magnificent Ambersons* was a different cup of tea; he had many other distractions.

"While he was shooting *The Magnificent Ambersons*, he was also doing a weekly one-hour Lady Esther radio show. Then, when we were halfway through shooting, war was declared and Orson was invited by the State Department to go to Brazil and make a film with the Brazilian people as part of the Good Neighbor Policy. He jumped at the opportunity. He had to report to Washington sometime in the latter part of February/early March to get a briefing about the trip and then go on to South America. That's all fine, but he got a wild notion early into January. He still owed RKO another film in his contract. I think he decided he'd like to

Orson Welles arrives in Brazil.

leave for Brazil free from any commitments. So he suddenly put a script he had on the shelf, *Journey Into Fear*, into work. He put Norman Foster in charge of directing it, he cast Joe Cotten, Dolores Del Rio and his associate producer, Jack Moss, in it, and decided that the only person to play the Turkish general was himself. So, for the last few weeks of shooting on *The Magnificent Ambersons*, he was directing it in the daytime and acting all night in *Journey Into Fear* [1942].

"Then he wasn't able to finish the editing with me because he had to be in Washington on a certain day. I needed some major decisions about the editing to be done and to get a hold of his narration. I packed my cans of film and met Orson at a small cartoon studio in Miami. We spent three days and nights working on it. The last I saw of Orson, he was leaving for Brazil. Jack Moss and I finished up the picture, and when we got an answer print, I was scheduled to fly down to Rio and show the film to Orson. A couple of days before I was supposed to take off, the U.S. government called an embargo on all civilian flights abroad. We sent the film down to him and received phone calls and cables from Orson with his suggestions, criticisms, and ideas for improvements.

"The studio got nervous. They wanted to see what they had, so they decided to have some previews. The first was a disaster; it just didn't play with the audience. They didn't care for the story, laughed at it and walked out of the film in droves. We were all in a state of shock. Then we took it out, without making any changes, to Pasadena, where the audience was supposed to appreciate more artistic things. We had the same experience there. The studio decided to cut it and pull it together, getting the booed spots out. When we finished that, we had to shoot some sequences to make the continuity work and put a new ending on it. I did one of the new scenes, the one where George comes in to see his mother about the letter Eugene has written. The new tag was done by Fred Fleck, who was the production manager on the film. And we finally had a preview in which it seemed to play.

"As a work of art and a cinematic achievement, it was undoubtedly a better film in its original length, but it just didn't play. I think the problem with *The Magnificent Ambersons* was, as with a lot of films, a matter of timing. When Orson started shooting, it was pre-war and nothing was going on. By the time it came out for previews, our whole country was all charged up with the war. Audiences just didn't have patience for this story of the Amberson family in Indianapolis, early in the century, and their problems. The changes were not a plot against Orson. We had a problem picture and he wasn't here to help us. Literally, I didn't see Orson from the time I saw him off down in Florida to go to South America until 1953. And over the years I only saw him four or five times. He never said to me directly, 'Hey you so-and-so, what did you do to my film?' I know he popped off about it in the press, but this is all high anxiety. I think the fact that it has come down through the years as a classic in its own right means that we didn't destroy everything that Orson did. I would be the first to say it."

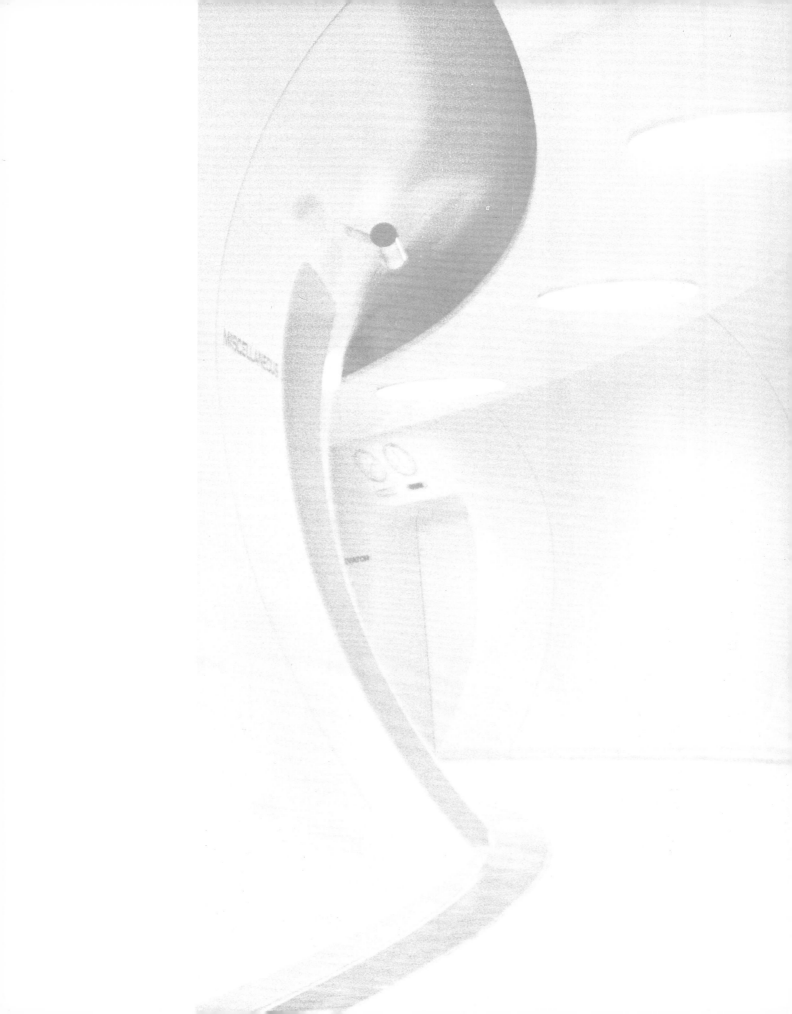

DIRECTOR

Kent Smith, Ann Carter, Jane Randolph, Eve March, Elizabeth Russell, and Julia Dean.

THE CURSE OF THE CAT PEOPLE
(RKO, 1944)

Directed by Robert Wise and Gunther von Fritsch. Produced by Val Lewton. Screenplay: DeWitt Bodeen. Director of Photography: Nicholas Musuraca. Music: Roy Webb. Musical Director: C. Bakaleinikoff. Assistant Director: Harry D'Arcy. Art Direction: Albert S. D'Agostino, Walter E. Keller. Set Decoration: Darrell Silvera, William Stevens. Costumes: Edward Stevenson. Makeup: Mel Berns. Sound: Francis M. Sarver, James G. Stewart. Film Editor: J. R. Whittredge. 70 minutes.

Cast: Simone Simon (Irena), Kent Smith (Oliver Reed), Jane Randolph (Alice Reed), Ann Carter (Amy Reed), Elizabeth Russell (Barbara Farren), Eve March (Miss Callahan), Julia Dean (Julia Farren), Erford Gage (Captain of Guard), Sir Lancelot (Edward), Joel Davis (Donald), Juanita Alvarez (Lois), Charley Bates (Jack), Gloria Donovan, Ginny Wren, and Linda Ann Bieber (Children), Sarah Selby (Miss Plunkett), Mel Sternlight (State Trooper).

Simone Simon and Ann Carter.

Six-year-old Amy's frequent escapes from reality cause great concern to her parents, Oliver and Alice Reed. Her abstractness reminds Oliver of his tragically deceased first wife, Irena, who believed herself to be a cat woman. Shunned by her schoolmates, Amy makes the acquaintance of Julia Farren, an aging actress who lives with her daughter Barbara in

Julia Dean and Ann Carter.

Eve March, Kent Smith, Jane Randolph.

an old mansion. Believing a ring Julia gave her has magic powers, Amy, feeling rejected, wishes for a friend. The playmate she conjures up takes on the likeness of Irena, whom Amy had seen in a photograph. The Reeds think everything is fine with their daughter until Amy finds another picture, this time of Irena and Oliver together, and asks her father if he knows her friend. Disturbed, Oliver tries to convince his daughter that Irena is just a product of her imagination, but Amy insists that she can see her friend in the garden and is punished. While Amy's teacher, Miss Callahan, explains to Oliver how lonely children fill the void for companionship with make-believe playmates, the child runs away. Barbara, jealous of her mother's affection for Amy, had threatened to kill the girl, so when Amy turns up at the Farren's, Julia tries to hide her. In an effort to climb the stairs, Julia dies. As Barbara comes close, Amy imagines she is Irena and embraces her. Amy's parents arrive, taking her back home, where Amy tells an understanding Oliver that she can still see Irena.

RW:

" I was editing *The Curse of the Cat People* in late summer/ early fall of 1943. I got a call from Val Lewton and Sid Rogell, the executive for the B-unit at RKO, on a Saturday, asking me to meet them for lunch. At the restaurant they said that they wanted me to take over direction on the following Monday. Gunther von Fritsch was a good director, but they couldn't speed him up. I was delighted, of course, but I also had a moment's hesitation because I had to go back that Saturday night and work with Gunther on the set. I felt uncomfortable about being on the set with him knowing that I was going to take over his job on Monday. When I expressed this to them, Rogell said, 'He's not going to be there Monday morning directing that film. Somebody else will. That can be you or somebody else, but he's not going to do it anymore. What is it going to be?' I knew it was the chance I had been waiting for and simply said, 'I'll be there.' Fortunately, I'd been on the set and knew the people I was going to work with. I only had a little problem with the production manager. I guess he was disappointed that he wasn't given the opportunity to take over and was a little tough with me the first couple of days. So much so that, at the end of the second day, I had to turn on him and tell him that if he didn't like it he could leave the picture. From then on he was fine."

MADEMOISELLE FIFI
(RKO, 1944)

Directed by Robert Wise. Produced by Val Lewton. Screenplay by Josef Mischel and Peter Ruric, based on the stories "Boule de Suif" and "Mademoiselle Fifi" by Guy de Maupassant. Director of Photography: Harry J. Wild. Music: Werner Heymann. Musical Director: C. Bakaleinikoff. Assistant Director: Sam Ruman. Costumes: Edward Stevenson. Art Direction: Albert S. D'Agostino, Walter E. Keller. Set Decoration: Darrell Silvera, Al Fields. Special Effects: Vernon L. Walker. Sound: Francis M. Sarver, James G. Stewart. Makeup: Mel Berns. Film Editor: J. R. Whittredge. 70 minutes.

Cast: Simone Simon (Elizabeth Rousset), John Emery (Jean Cornudet), Kurt Kreuger (Lieutenant von Eyrick, known as Mademoiselle Fifi), Alan Napier (Count de Breville), Helen Freeman (Countess de Breville), Jason Robards (Wine Wholesaler), Norma Varden (Wholesaler's Wife), Romaine Callender (Manufacturer), Fay Helm (Manufacturer's Wife), Edmund Glover (Young Priest), Charles Waldron (Curé of Cleresville), Mayo Newhall (Mr. Follenvie), Lillian Bronson (Mrs. Follenvie), Alan Ward (Coach Driver), Dawn Kennedy (Maid), William von Wymetal (Major), Max Willenz (Captain), Marc Cramer (Lieutenant), John Good (Fritz), Allan Lee (Coach Driver), Frank Mayo (Sergeant at Inn), Margaret Landry (Eva), Rosemary LaPlanche (Blondini), Marie Lund (Helene), Margie Stewart (Pamela), Violet Wilson (Aunt Marie), Tom Burton and Steve Winston (Uhlans), Paul Marion (Devoir), Ed Allen (Soldier), Richard Drumm (German Sentry), Victor Cutler (Soldier Waiter).

John Emery and Simone Simon.

France during the Franco-Prussian War, 1870. With a pass obtained from the Prussian authorities, a young French laundress, Elizabeth Rousset, boards a coach in Rouen that will take her to her hometown of Cleresville. The other passengers are three affluent couples, a revolutionary named Cornudet, and a priest on his way to replace the Curé of Cleresville. Cornudet and the priest are the only ones to show some sympathy for

Elizabeth. The others cold-shoulder her because of her social standing and staunchly patriotic opinions. The coach stops for the night in Totes, and the passengers are received at the inn by Lieutenant von Eyrick, a Prussian officer nicknamed Mademoiselle Fifi. Knowing that Elizabeth adamantly refuses to mingle with the Prussian invaders, von Eyrick invites her for supper and she declines. The next morning, the travelers are informed that they will be detained until Elizabeth changes her mind. At first, her companions back up her decision, but as time passes, they talk her into sacrificing her principles for the sake of the group. After being humbled by von Eyrick, the laundress is further humiliated when the three couples treat her with open disdain.

Helen Freeman, Romaine Callender, Mayo Newhall, Jason Robards, John Emery, Lillian Bronson, Norma Varden, Alan Napier, and Fay Helm.

Working at her aunt's laundry shop in Cleresville, Elizabeth is forced to attend a party at the Prussian headquarters, where von Eyrick again tries to degrade her. Elizabeth kills the Prussian and flees, finding refuge in the Cleresville church. Like his predecessor, the priest had promised to keep the church's bell silent until the first blow for the freedom of France was struck. With von Eyrick dead, the bell tolls again.

Simone Simon, John Emery, and Edmund Glover.

Simone Simon, Romaine
Callender, Jason Robards,
Norma Varden, Fay Helm,
Helen Freeman, John Emery,
and Alan Napier.

RW:

" Because those were low-budget films, we had to stretch our imagination and get results without too much to work with. How we staged them, how we lit them, how we placed our camera was to get strong, effective results without having the material at hand. One of the aspects of filmmaking that I'm sure I learned from Val Lewton was the importance of the right look of the picture. When doing a period film, he would go back to the artists of the time and get prints of their key works to use as a direction in terms of composition, lighting, sets, costumes, and character types. When I did *Mademoiselle Fifi*, he said, 'We must get Daumier sketches.' We got those and hung them up on the wall. A lot of details of sets, how things and people looked, the clothes and hairstyles came from those Daumier prints. When Mark Robson did *Bedlam*, they got a lot of ideas from Hogarth. That became something I always remembered and used from time to time: to pick up on an artist of the period and how he saw things."

Wise rehearses a scene with Simone Simon and Kurt Kreuger.

THE BODY SNATCHER

(RKO, 1945)

Directed by Robert Wise. Produced by Val Lewton. Executive Producer: Jack J. Gross. Screenplay: Philip MacDonald and Carlos Keith [Val Lewton], based on a story by Robert Louis Stevenson. Director of Photography: Robert De Grasse. Music: Roy Webb. Musical Direction: C. Bakaleinikoff. Assistant Director: Harry Scott. Art Direction: Albert S. D'Agostino, Walter E. Keller. Set Decoration: Darrell Silvera, John Sturtevant. Costumes: Renie. Sound: Bailey Fesler, Terry Kellum. Film Editor: J. R. Whittredge. 77 minutes.

Cast: Boris Karloff (John Gray), Bela Lugosi (Joseph), Henry Daniell (Dr. MacFarlane), Edith Atwater (Meg MacFarlane), Russell Wade (Fettes), Rita Corday (Mrs. Marsh), Sharyn Moffett (Georgina Marsh), Donna Lee (Street Singer), Robert Clarke (Richardson), Carl Kent (Gilchrist), Bill Williams (Student), Jack Welch (Boy), Larry Wheat (Salesman), Mary Gordon (Mrs. McBride), Jim Moran (Horse Trader), Aina Constant (Maid).

Henry Daniell and Boris Karloff.

BS-52

Rita Corday, Edith Atwater, Sharyn Moffett, and Boris Karloff.

*E*dinburgh, 1831. A renowned surgeon, Dr. MacFarlane, refuses to perform a difficult operation on a paralytic child, Georgina Marsh, alleging his total commitment to teaching. One of his pupils, Fettes, tells the doctor that he won't be able to pursue his education for lack of funds and is made an assistant. Among Fettes' duties is to receive the corpses supplied by cabman and grave-robber John Gray for the anatomy classes. Gray had once been sentenced to jail to keep MacFarlane's name out of a scandalous trial involving grave-robbing, and the cabman uses this incident to constrain the doctor into attempting Georgina's cure. MacFarlane requests a body for research before the surgery and Gray obliges by killing a street singer, much to Fettes' dismay. The operation is a success, but still Georgina refuses to walk. Gray's next victim is Joseph, a servant at the medical school, who had tried to blackmail him. Resolved to put an end to Gray's maleficent hold over him, MacFarlane kills the cabman, disposing of the body outside Edinburgh. Meanwhile, Georgina takes her first steps. Exultant, Fettes finds MacFarlane at an inn and breaks the news. Free from Gray's evil influence and with renewed confidence in his own abilities, MacFarlane takes his assistant to steal a freshly buried cadaver so that they can continue their studies. Driving back through a storm, MacFarlane imagines the body next to him to be Gray's. In panic, he loses control of the carriage and dies in a crash.

Boris Karloff.

RW:

" Boris Karloff was a lovely man, the complete opposite of what he played on the screen. He was a very gentle, educated, well-read, sensitive man, and he was very keen about the movie. He felt that the role of Gray was a chance for him to prove that he was something more than just a monster out to scare people, that he was an actor. Because of the nature of the part, and the duels he had with the doctor played by Henry Daniell, he put his heart and soul into it. I love those scenes between the two of them. Henry Daniell was a brilliant actor, and Karloff knew it was going to be a challenge. I think he held his own very well with Daniell and did a marvelous job. He worked very hard, even though he was having back problems.

"Bela Lugosi was an afterthought. His character was not in the original script, but the studio felt that it would be great if we had the names Karloff and Lugosi on the marquees. Val didn't like the idea. He tried to talk them out of it, but wasn't able to. So he worked him in by creating the role of the porter. Lugosi was really not well at the time. I had to be very gentle with him, almost nursing him through the few scenes he had.

"We used sections of the old standing sets for *The Hunchback of Notre Dame* at the RKO ranch—one for the graveyard with the old lady and the dog, another for the

Russell Wade, Boris Karloff, and Bela Lugosi.

Boris Karloff, Bela Lugosi, and Henry Daniell.

marvelous shot where the singer walks down through the arch into the dark followed by Gray. That was one of Val's talents—a great facility for seeing things that were lying around and working them into the scripts. He made a film called *The Ghost Ship*, which stemmed from the fact that RKO made a picture that had a freighter in it. Val saw that and said, 'Let's write a suspense story around that ship.' He created the whole thing to use those sets. I think our budget for sets on some of these pictures was $10,000 or under. Mostly we made adjustments in existing sets.

"Val was tremendously supportive to those of us who were just starting as directors. He never interfered with you on the set, he was only helpful. I remember one time when I was shooting *The Body Snatcher* and I was getting a little behind. The studio was sending me messages all the time: 'You're going slow.' 'You shot too much yesterday.' Val would always see the rushes with the front-office people and later would come down to the set and tell how the rushes were. One day he came and said, 'The rushes look fine; we loved them. They want you to pick up, you're behind schedule. Now I tell you, go ahead and make your film.' That's the kind of man he was. He warned me as they wanted him to, then gave me a pat on the back and told me to go ahead and make my film."

A GAME OF DEATH
(RKO, 1945)

Directed by Robert Wise. Produced by Herman Schlom. Executive Producer: Sid Rogell. Screenplay: Norman Houston, based on the story "The Most Dangerous Game" by Richard Connell. Director of Photography: J. Roy Hunt. Music: Paul Sawtell. Musical Director: C. Bakaleinikoff. Special Effects: Vernon L. Walker. Assistant Director: Doran Cox. Gowns: Renie. Art Direction: Albert S. D'Agostino, Lucius Croxton. Set Decoration: Darrell Silvera, James Altwies. Sound: Phillip Mitchell, James G. Stewart. Film Editor: J. R. Whittredge. 72 minutes.

Cast: John Loder (Don Rainsford), Audrey Long (Ellen Trowbridge), Edgar Barrier (Eric Kreiger), Russell Wade (Robert Trowbridge), Russell Hicks (Whitney), Jason Robards (Captain), Gene Stutenroth (Pleshke), Noble Johnson (Carib), Robert Clarke (Helmsman), Edmund Glover (Quartermaster), Bruce Edwards (Collins), Jimmy Jordan (Steward), Vic Romito (Mongol), Jimmy Dime (Bulgar).

Gene Stutenroth, Edgar Barrier, and John Loder.

* Other versions: *The Most Dangerous Game* (1932, directed by Ernest B. Schoedsack and Irving Pichel); *Run for the Sun* (1956, directed by Roy Boulting).

Don Rainsford, a famous sportsman and writer, is the sole survivor of a shipwreck on a rocky, remote coast. He seeks refuge in a castle on the island owned by Eric Kreiger, a big-game hunter who lives in luxury accompanied by his servants and a pack of bloodhounds. Over dinner, Kreiger introduces Rainsford to two other guests, Ellen Trowbridge and her brother Robert, themselves victims of an earlier shipwreck. Instigated by a suspicious Ellen, Rainsford breaks into Kreiger's trophy room, where he finds showcases containing preserved human heads. As it turns out, Kreiger is a maniac who, tired of hunting animals, uses human beings as quarry. To keep him supplied, he places false navigation lights off the coast, luring boats into certain doom. In spite of Rainsford's efforts, Robert becomes the deranged man's unfortunate next prey. With Robert dead, Rainsford challenges Kreiger into hunting himself and Ellen. They are given ten minutes' head start into the jungle before Kreiger begins his relentless pursuit. A hunter himself, Rainsford uses his cunning and pretends to be dead. Kreiger takes Ellen to the castle. The following morning, Rainsford reappears, kills the servants, mortally wounds Kreiger, and rescues Ellen.

RW:

" When you're under contract like I was, you may turn down one or two films until finally they say, 'Now come on, you're under contract here and you have to do it.' I did have layoff periods. At one time I had six weeks taken off the end of one period and twelve weeks from the beginning of the next one. I spent almost five months sitting around the house and climbing the wall. In other words, the original contract, what they called the 'twenty out of twenty-six weeks,' paid you a guaranteed twenty weeks, but they could lay you off for six weeks without payment. After two of those contracts, you went to yearly contracts in which they would guarantee you forty weeks' pay, but they could lay you off for up to twelve weeks without pay. So I had a period of eighteen weeks without income except my social security. That's why I did films like *A Game of Death* and *Criminal Court*. Also, I was still learning. You don't learn when you're sitting at home. Everything you do should add to your repertoire, your knowledge of how to do things.

Edgar Barrier.

"*A Game of Death* was a remake of *The Most Dangerous Game*, and I wasn't terribly keen about doing remakes. What bothered me was the fact that I had to run the old picture to see how I could utilize some shots of Great Danes going through the swamps and the jungle. The studio wanted me to use those shots because working with dogs can be expensive. I found it very annoying later on when I was actually shooting the film. As we went into different sequences, I could not help thinking about the sequence that was in the old film. It felt like somebody looking over my shoulders. The same thing happened when I made *So Big* in 1953, and I haven't done a remake since."

Noble Johnson, Edgar Barrier, and John Loder.

CRIMINAL COURT
(RKO, 1946)

Directed by Robert Wise. Produced by Martin Mooney. Executive Producer: Sid Rogell. Screenplay: Lawrence Kimble, based on a story by Earl Felton. Director of Photography: Frank Redman. Music: Paul Sawtell. Musical Director: C. Bakaleinikoff. Songs: "I Couldn't Sleep a Wink Last Night" and "A Lovely Way to Spend an Evening" by Jimmy McHugh and Harold Adamson. Special Effects: Russell A. Cully. Art Direction: Albert S. D'Agostino, Lucius Croxton. Set Decoration: Darrell Silvera, Michael Orenbach. Sound: Francis M. Sarver, Roy Granville. Film Editor: Robert Swink. Former Title: "Manhattan Miracle." 63 minutes.

Cast: Tom Conway (Steve Barnes), Martha O'Driscoll (Georgia Gale), June Clayworth (Joan Mason), Robert Armstrong (Vic Wright), Addison Richards (Distric Attorney Gordon), Pat Gleason (Joe West), Steve Brodie (Frankie Wright), Robert Warwick (Marquette), Phil Warren (Bill Brannegan), Joe Devlin (Brownie), Lee Bonnell (Gil Lambert), Robert Clarke (Dance Director).

Steve Barnes is an eminent lawyer of rather flamboyant methods. As part of his campaign to be elected district attorney, he makes every effort to expose the crime syndicate headed by Marquette. So it is with great embarrassment that he is told by his fiancée, Georgia Gale, that she landed a job as a singer at a nightclub whose proprietor, Vic Wright, is a member of Marquette's clique. In an attempt to blackmail Barnes into not divulging incriminating evidence, Wright invites the lawyer to his establishment. He threatens Barnes with a gun, the two fight, and Wright is killed accidentally. Barnes flees the scene of the crime without re-

Tom Conway and Martha O'Driscoll.

alizing that the incident was witnessed by his own secretary, Joan Mason, who also acted as Wright's informant. Later, Georgia walks into Wright's office, finds his body, and is caught by Wright's brother, Frankie.

Tom Conway and Martha O'Driscoll.

Charged with the murder, Georgia will stand trial, despite Barnes' attempts to convince the police that he was responsible. Marquette offers to provide Barnes with an eyewitness if Barnes renounces his political ambitions, but Georgia stops him from accepting the deal. During the trial, Barnes sees all the evidence pointing to Georgia as the culprit until he remembers a remark made by Joan that pinpoints her having seen the crime. Called to the stand, Joan breaks down and confesses. Georgia is acquitted.

RW:

"*Criminal Court* runs sixty-three minutes. To tell so much plot in so short a time, the B-pictures had fully developed stories and well-rounded screenplays. It always fascinates me how pictures over the years have grown in length. When I was a film editor and after, we considered a normal film about one hour and a half maximum. If you got a first cut that came in at about one hour forty-five minutes, you would worry that it was going to be too long. I'm not just talking about B-pictures, which were about one hour, one hour and ten minutes long. I'm talking about bigger pictures with bigger stars. Take *My Favorite Wife*, which I edited, as an example. It's an outstanding film with Cary Grant, Irene Dunne, Gail Patrick, and Randolph Scott, and it runs eighty-eight minutes. Now you have two hours, two hours and ten minutes, two hours and twenty minutes, and, of course, the roadshows got up to three hours. I don't know what happened to us in our storytelling process—it seems to have inflated over the years."

BORN TO KILL
(RKO, 1947)

Directed by Robert Wise. Produced by Herman Schlom. Executive Producer: Sid Rogell. Screenplay by Eve Greene and Richard Macaulay, based on the novel "Deadlier Than the Male" by James Gunn. Director of Photography: Robert De Grasse. Music: Paul Sawtell. Musical Director: C. Bakaleinikoff. Special Effects: Russell A. Cully. Art Direction Albert S. D'Agostino, Walter E. Keller. Set Decoration: Darrell Silvera, John Sturtevant. Costumes: Edward Stevenson. Sound: Robert H. Guhl, Roy Granville. Film Editor: Les Millbrook. Former Title: "Deadlier Than the Male." 92 minutes.

Cast: Claire Trevor (Helen Trent), Lawrence Tierney (Sam Wild), Walter Slezak (Albert Arnett), Philip Terry (Fred Grover), Audrey Long (Georgia Staples), Elisha Cook, Jr. (Marty Waterman), Isabel Jewell (Laury Palmer), Esther Howard (Mrs. Kraft), Kathryn Card (Grace), Tony Barrett (Danny), Grandon Rhodes (Inspector Wilson), Sam Lufkin, Sayre Dearing, Sammy Shack, and Joe Dixon (Crap Dealers), Ruth Brennan (Sally), Tom Noonan (Bellboy), Al Murphy (Cab Driver), Phil Warren (Chauffeur), Ben Frommer (Delivery Boy), Netta Packer (Mrs. Perth), Lee Frederick (Desk Clerk), Demetrius Alexis (Maitre d'), Martha Hyer (Maid), Beatrice Maude (Cook), Ellen Corby (Second Maid), Jean Fenwick (Margaret Macy), Reverend Neal Dodd (Clergyman), Napoleon Whiting (Porter), Perc Launders (Detective Bryson), Stanley Stone (Train Conductor), Jason Robards (Conductor).

*O*n the night she is leaving Reno after obtaining a divorce, Helen Trent finds the murdered bodies of Laury Palmer and her friend Danny, but doesn't report the fact to the police. On the train, she meets Sam Wild, the killer, to whom she feels irresistibly drawn. Arriving in San Francisco, Sam follows Helen to her foster sister Georgia's house, where he learns that Helen is engaged to wealthy Fred Grover, and turns his attention to Georgia, a rich heiress. Soon after, Sam and Georgia marry, with Sam's devoted friend Marty as best man. Distressed, Helen purposely gives a clue to Albert Arnett, a private detective hired by Laury's beneficiary, elderly Mrs. Kraft, to find Laury's murderer. Georgia and Sam return early from their honeymoon, quarreling about Georgia's refusal to let Sam run a newspa-

Claire Trevor, Elisha Cook, Jr., and Lawrence Tierney.

Esther Howard and Claire Trevor.

Lawrence Tierney and Claire Trevor.

Esther Howard and Walter Slezak.

per she owns. Helen cannot resist Sam's advances and decides to buy Arnett's silence. In his psychotic mind, Sam imagines that Marty is having an affair with Helen. Marty lures Mrs. Kraft to a deserted beach, but, as he prepares to do her in, he is killed by Sam. Mrs. Kraft escapes only to be coerced by Helen into dropping the case. Feeling unable to curb her depraved attraction to Sam, Helen informs on him. Sam shoots Helen just as the police break in to kill him.

RW:

" The original book was called *Deadlier Than the Male*, and anybody who's seen the film knows how meaningful that is. But having Lawrence Tierney in the part, the studio thought it was important to get something more striking in the title. I was never happy about the change. *Deadlier Than the Male* was perfect for that story in which the lady played by Claire Trevor turns out to be just that.

"*Born to Kill* was a middle-ground film, someplace between a B- and an A-picture. I had more money, more time, and a very good cast. It got pretty badly attacked at the time but, by today's standards, it is very mild. Today's movies usually show so much blood and gore in graphic detail and slow motion, literally rubbing the audience's nose in this sort of gruesome stuff, that *Born to Kill* seems rather soft now. In terms of the dynamism of the story, however, it holds up well. I pushed very hard and was very instrumental in getting it done. I thought a lot of it was just excellent."

MYSTERY IN MEXICO
(RKO, 1948)

Directed by Robert Wise. Produced by Sid Rogell. Associate Producer: Joseph Noriega. Screenplay: Lawrence Kimble. Story: Muriel Roy Bolton. Director of Photography: Jack Draper. Music: Paul Sawtell. Musical Director: C. Bakaleinikoff. Assistant Director: Jaime Contreras. Art Direction: Gunther Gerzso. Gowns: Renie. Special Effects: Russell A. Cully. Sound: Jose B. Carles, Fred L. Granville. Film Editor: Samuel E. Beetley. 65 minutes.

    Cast: William Lundigan (Steve Hastings), Jacqueline White (Victoria Ames), Ricardo Cortez (Joe Norcross), Tony Barrett (Carlos), Jacqueline Dalya (Dolores), Walter Reed (Glenn Ames), Jose Torvay (Swigart), Jaime Jimenez (Pancho Gomez), Antonio Frausto (Pancho's Father), Dolores Camerillo (Pancho's Mother), Eduardo Casado (Commandant Rodriguez), Thalia Draper (Florecita), Carlos Muzquiz (Luis Otero), Freddie Romero (Jose), Alfonso Jimenez (Lopez), Conchita Gentil (Benny's Mother), Lilia Plancarte (Benny's Sister), Suzi Crandall and Marilyn Mercer (Flight Hostesses), William Forrest (Powers).

*I*nsurance investigator Glenn Ames disappears in Mexico City with a necklace worth $200,000. Central Trust Insurance Company sends Steve Hastings to tag along with Ames' sister, Victoria, who is leaving for Mexico. He makes her acquaintance on the plane, without disclosing his identity. Victoria is hired as a singer at the Versailles nightclub, owned by Joe Norcross, where her brother posed as a bartender. With the aid of Carlos, a friendly taxi driver, Hastings tries to locate Benny, a barman at the same nightclub, who seems to know about Glenn Ames. The next day, Hastings learns that Benny has been killed in a car accident. Hastings tells Victoria about his job. A boy brings Victoria a message from her brother, and Carlos accompanies them to the boy's house, where

Ricardo Cortez and Jacqueline White.

they find an ailing Ames. Carlos, pretending to go fetch a doctor, calls Norcross. Hastings overhears the phone conversation, gets knocked out, and wakes up when Glenn Ames is being beaten into confessing where he hid the necklace. Given a false lead by Ames, Norcross sends Carlos to Victoria's hotel room, which alerts a policeman standing guard at the door. The police go to the house where Ames is held and kill Norcross and Carlos. Hastings and Victoria stay in Mexico to get married.

RW:

66 At that time, RKO owned forty-nine percent of the Churubusco Studios in Mexico City. I was asked to go down there and make a film using all their people. I didn't take anybody from the States at all. It was a very enjoyable experience for me, my first living out of the country and my only one working with an almost exclusively foreign crew. Originally we planned to do all the post-production down there, but we got a little behind and it was decided to bring the film back to Hollywood and do all the finishing up— editing, music score, sound effects—at RKO. Because we went somewhat over budget, I think, in the final analysis, it seemed to cost as much to make the film down there as it would have cost here. The studio wanted to know if it could make more reasonably priced movies in Mexico, and it turned out not to be so."

BLOOD ON THE MOON
(RKO, 1948)

Directed by Robert Wise. Produced by Theron Warth. Executive Producer: Sid Rogell. Screenplay: Lillie Hayward, based on the novel by Luke Short. Adaptation: Harold Shumate and Luke Short. Director of Photography: Nicholas Musuraca. Music: Roy Webb. Musical Director: C. Bakaleinikoff. Gowns: Edward Stevenson. Special Effects: Russell A. Cully. Art Direction: Albert S. D'Agostino, Walter E. Keller. Set Decoration: Darrell Silvera, James Altwies. Makeup Supervision: Gordon Bau. Sound: John L. Cass, Terry Kellum. Assistant Director: Maxwell O. Henry. Film Editor: Samuel E. Beetley. 88 minutes.

Cast: Robert Mitchum (Jim Garry), Barbara Bel Geddes (Amy Lufton), Robert Preston (Tate Riling), Walter Brennan (Kris Barden), Phyllis Thaxter (Carol Lufton), Frank Faylen (Jake Pindalest), Tom Tully (John Lufton), Charles McGraw (Milo Sweet), Clifton Young (Joe Shotten), Tom Tyler (Frank Reardan), George Cooper (Fred Barden), Richard Powers (Ted Elser), Bud Osborne (Cap Willis), Zon Murray (Nels Titterton), Robert Bray (Bart Daniels), Al Ferguson (Chet Avery), Ben Corbett (Mitch Moten), Joe Devlin (Barney), Erville Alderson (Settlmeir), Robert Malcolm (Sheriff Manker), Chris-Pin Martin (Bartender at Commissary), Ruth Brennan (Townswoman), Harry Carey, Jr., Hal Taliaferro and Al Murphy (Cowboys), Iron Eyes Cody (Toma).

Walter Brennan, Robert Mitchum, and George Cooper.

In the late 1860s, wandering cowboy Jim Garry is summoned by his friend Tate Riling. On his way to see Riling, Garry is picked up by cattleman John Lufton, who is waging a war against the local homesteaders. Convinced of Garry's neutrality in the conflict, Lufton gives the stranger a letter to be delivered to his family. After delivering the note to Lufton's fiery daughter, Amy, Garry meets up with Riling and learns that Riling needs him as a gunman to help in a crooked scheme. In collusion with corrupt Indian agent Jake Pindalest, Riling, who hopes to force Lufton into selling his cattle for a very low price, uses the farmers to stop Lufton from moving his herd out of Indian reservation land. A false tip-off as to when Lufton would move his cattle, contained in the letter Garry delivered to Amy, is passed on to Riling by his lover, Lufton's other daughter, Carol. The cattleman's plan almost succeeds, but Riling's men stampede

George Cooper, Walter Brennan, and Barbara Bel Geddes.

the herd back onto the reservation. Disgusted with his friend's methods, Garry changes sides, saves Lufton from being killed, and slugs it out with Riling in a tavern. Garry then abducts Pindalest so that Lufton can sell his cattle in a legitimate market. Riling tracks Garry down, freeing Pindalest. Wounded, Garry holes up with Amy in homesteader Kris Barden's cabin. In the gunfight that follows, Garry kills Riling and takes Pindalest alive. The range war comes to an end when the homesteaders realize they were being manipulated by Riling.

Barbara Bel Geddes and Robert Mitchum.

RW:

" When I got my chance to direct, I signed the standard seven-year contract with RKO. My first picture starred Simone Simon, and she was represented by Famous Artists, a big agency at the time. She talked to them and they approached me about handling me. I signed with them with the understanding that they would not take any commission from me until I had bettered my deal. That went on for a few years. They never did anything for me particularly, but that didn't bother me. We were getting *Blood on the Moon* ready for shooting when I got a call from Sid Rogell. He said, 'You ought to check in on your agency.

Robert Preston and Robert Mitchum slug it out.

You got this project that Dore Schary likes and wants to do, and they went up there in the front office undercutting you, trying to sell another director and a couple of stars that they have.' They were trying to make a package deal with James Stewart and somebody else, with Jacques Tourneur directing it. At that time Jacques was getting $75,000 a picture, big money. But Schary, who was then head of production at RKO, wouldn't hear of it. He said, 'It's Wise's picture. He's been working on it, he's going to do it.' That's the kind of man Dore Schary was—very straight, very honest. Of course, I left Famous Artists right away."

Robert Mitchum and Robert Preston.

THE SET-UP
(RKO, 1949)

Directed by Robert Wise. Produced by Richard Goldstone. Screenplay: Art Cohn, based on the poem by Joseph Moncure March. Director of Photography: Milton Krasner. Musical Direction: C. Bakaleinikoff. Fight Sequences by John Indrisano. Assistant Director: Edward Killy. Art Direction: Albert S. D'Agostino, Jack Okey. Set Decoration: Darrell Silvera, James Altwies. Makeup Supervision: Gordon Bau. Sound: Phil Brigandi, Clem Portman. Film Editor: Roland Gross. 72 minutes.

Cast: Robert Ryan (Stoker Thompson), Audrey Totter (Julie), George Tobias (Tiny), Alan Baxter (Little Boy), Wallace Ford (Gus), Percy Helton (Red), Hal Fieberling (Tiger Nelson), Darryl Hickman (Shanley), Kenny O'Morrison (Moore), James Edwards (Luther Hawkins), David Clarke (Gunboat Johnson), Phillip Pine (Souza), Edwin Max (Danny), Dave Fresco (Mickey), William E. Green (Doctor), Abe Dinovitch (Ring Caller), Jack Chase (Hawkins' Second), Mike Lally, Arthur Sullivan, William McCarther, and Gene Delmont (Handlers), Herbert Anderson and Jack Raymond (Husbands), Helen Brown and Costance Worth (Wives), Walter Ridge (Manager), Jess Kirkpatrick, and Paul Dubov (Gamblers), Frank Richards (Bat), Jack Stoney (Nelson's Second), Archie Leonard (Blind Man), John Butler, Ralph Volke, Tony Merrill, Carl Sklover, Sam Shack, Herman Bodel, Andy Carillo, Charles Sullivan, Al Rehin, Tom Noonan, Dan Foster, Everett Smith, Brian O'Hara, and Donald Kerr (Men), Lillian Castle, Frances Mack, and Ruth Brennan (Women), Lynn Millan (Bunny), Bernard Gorcey (Tobacco Man), Charles Wagenheim (Hamburger Man), Billy Snyder (Barker), W. J. O'Brien (Pitchman), Frank Mills (Photographer), Bobby Henshaw (Announcer), Dwight Martin (Glutton), Noble "Kid" Chissel (Handler), Ben Moselle (Referee), Arthur Weegee Fellig (Timekeeper).

Jury Award at the Cannes Film Festival.

Robert Ryan, George Tobias, David Clarke.

At 35, Stoker Thompson is a prizefighter past his prime, condemned to the bottom of the bill in tanktown arenas. His loving wife, Julie, would like to see him give up the racket, settle down, and possibly start a small business of his own. They argue in their cheap hotel room before Stoker leaves for the arena, reaffirming his optimistic belief that he can still punch his way to the top. His manager, Tiny, is convinced Stoker will be defeated in the bout against a younger opponent, Tiger Nelson, and accepts fifty dollars from Nelson's owner, Little Boy, to make sure Stoker takes a dive. In the ring, Stoker and Nelson engage in a fierce battle. Clinging to this one chance to reestablish himself, Stoker attacks his adversary furiously. In the third round, Nelson keeps telling him it is time to end the fight, and Stoker, who had not been told about Little Boy's bribe, realizes there has been a frame-up. Refusing to throw the fight, he goes on, knocking Nelson out in the fourth round. After being threatened by Little Boy in the dressing room, Stoker tries to escape through a side door, but is caught by Nelson and two of Little Boy's men. They smash his right hand, putting an end to his dreams. Worried, Julie looks through the window of her room and sees her beleaguered husband on the pavement. As she comforts him, her sorrow at the cruelty inflicted on him mixes with the hopes for a better future that she is sure lies ahead for them.

Cast and crew of **The Set-Up**. *Seated: producer Richard Goldstone (with glasses), Hal Fieberling, Wise, Robert Ryan, technical advisor Johnny Indrisano, and George Tobias. Cinematographer Milton Krasner is standing next to camera in dark vest.*

RW:

      " Here was a boxing film that for once wasn't Madison Square Garden and the championship belt. I spent night after night doing research at the arenas around town. There was a little crummy one down in Long Beach I went to several times on their fight night. I would get down there early and go to the dressing rooms and watch the fighters, their managers, and handlers coming in from the street. I would watch a whole evening of their actions and activities, making notes, getting pictures and lots of ideas. On other nights, I would watch the fights and see how the handlers act in the corners, what went on between the rounds, watch the crowds, pick up little pieces of business. The screenwriter, Art Cohn, knew the boxing game and brought so much to the film in terms of what went on behind the scenes. Many characters that he indicated in the script are right out of his experiences. For instance, the blind man was an actual character he saw in the weekly fights in San Francisco—a blind man who came in with a companion who explained to him what was going on. Other characters I added myself, out of my weeks of research. Like the man who has the radio tuned to the ballgame while he watches the fight, and the man with the cigar, never quite getting it in his mouth during the excitement of a round.

Vincent Graeff and Robert Ryan.

      "The film was shot almost entirely in the studio. The empty arena where Stoker is caught in a kind of spider web was a real one, but all the other fight stuff was done at RKO. The fight scenes were planned, rehearsed, and choreographed by Johnny Indrisano, who had been a professional fighter himself. He came to Hollywood in the mid-'30s and made a career out of staging fights. He took Bob Ryan and his opponent and rehearsed with them extensively before we went on to shoot it. When shooting a fight, you can only do twenty, thirty seconds at a time because it's too wearying. You rehearse a section until it's right, then you go on to the next section. All the movements are in a sense choreographed. We spent about a week on the fight. I used three cameras: one covering the whole ring, another covering the two of them, and a hand-held camera. I told the operator of the latter, 'Get all the little

Audrey Totter and Robert Ryan.

closeup bits and pieces that you can.' He got some marvelous close shots of gloves hitting and sweat flying off. When it came to editing that sequence, we had so much film that the editor, Roland Gross, couldn't come up with a cut that satisfied me, so I did it myself. It was the last actual editing of any consequence that I've done.

"*The Set-Up* was the first time I used storyboards, and the start of my association with sketch artist Maurice Zuberano, with whom I worked on many other films. We waited so long for the go-ahead from the studio that we were able to sketch the entire picture before I started to shoot. *The Set-Up* was shot closer to the actual sketches than any picture I ever did. In my early pictures, when I had no sketch artist, I would go into the set before we started filming and walk around and study. When we got to the shooting, I would be in the studio between five and six in the morning, long before the crew came in. I'd go onto the dark stages, turn the lights on, take the covers off the props and furniture, and work with my viewfinder, playing the parts, studying the sets, making notes where I wanted the camera to be, where I wanted the actors to move.

Robert Ryan, David Clarke and Wallace Ford.

George Tobias and Robert Ryan.

Robert Ryan.

Robert Ryan and Hal Fieberling.

Hal Fieberling and Robert Ryan.

"The only interest Howard Hughes had at all in the film was who was to play the leading lady. We had originally thought of Joan Blondell. She had done a film called *Nightmare Alley* in which she played Tyrone Power's wife, and she was a little blowzy and very earthy. We had always seen Stoker's wife as wife and mother to him, so we thought that the Blondell we saw in *Nightmare Alley* would be just right. With some trepidation, we threw this idea to Sid Rogell. We were hesitant, thinking he would not buy this at all, but, unexpectedly, he said it was a marvelous idea. The next day he called us back and said, 'Here's Hughes' answer to that suggestion: What's wrong with those guys? Blondell looks like she was shot out of the wrong end of a cannon.' That was the start of several weeks of this going back and forth. We would send up lists. We were always trying to reach for somebody of that quality, people like Sylvia Sidney, for instance. All were turned down by him. Instead, he sent lists of all the models, all the sexpots in town. They were absolutely wrong. I don't think he ever read the script; all he could see for the woman's part was some kind of beauty. We were getting desperate, shooting was to start in two or three days. Finally, on one of the lists we found Audrey Totter. I think she did an excellent job.

"*The Set-Up* was a labor of love for all of us. It got generally good reviews here, but there was another picture that came out at the same time that was Madison Square Garden and the championship belt, *Champion*, directed by my friend Mark Robson, and it got most of the publicity. But *The Set-Up* got outstanding reviews, especially in Europe, where it won an award at the Cannes Film Festival. I remember when I left RKO and signed to go to 20th Century-Fox, I met Billy Wilder and Jean Negulesco there and they said to me, 'If *The Set-Up* had been done in France or Italy, it would have gotten all the raves in the world from the critics here.' It's one of my favorites and continues to be thought of as maybe the best boxing picture ever made."

THREE SECRETS

(Warner Bros./United States Pictures, 1950)

Directed by Robert Wise. Produced by Milton Sperling. Written by Martin Rackin and Gina Kaus. Director of Photography: Sid Hickox. Music: David Buttolph. Orchestration: Maurice de Packh. Dialogue Director: Anthony Jowitt. Special Effects: William McGann (director), Edwin DuPar. Assistant Director: Russell Saunders. Art Direction: Charles H. Clarke. Set Decoration: Fred M. McLean. Wardrobe: Leah Rhodes. Makeup Artist: Perc Westmore. Sound: Charles Lang. Film Editor: Thomas Reilly. Former Title: "The Rock Bottom." 98 minutes.

Cast: Eleanor Parker (Susan Chase), Patricia Neal (Phyllis Horn), Ruth Roman (Ann Lawrence), Frank Lovejoy (Bob Duffy), Leif Erickson (Bill Chase), Ted de Corsia (Del Prince), Edmon Ryan (Hardin), Larry Keating (Mark Harrison), Katherine Warren (Mrs. Connors), Arthur Franz (Paul Radin), Duncan Richardson (Johnny).

A private plane crashes on a Sierra peak and aerial photographs reveal that the sole survivor is a five-year-old boy, Johnny, the foster son of a couple killed in the wreck. As a rescue party is organized to climb up the inhospitable cliff, three women of disparate backgrounds converge at the foot of the mountain. A newspaper had disclosed that the child was adopted at a certain institution, and each one of the women believes that she could be his real mother since all three had turned over a newly born boy to that same foundling home. The reasons leading to their giving up their babies are shown in flashbacks. Susan Chase's pregnancy was the result of a romance with a soldier engaged to another woman. A hardboiled reporter, Phyllis Horn sacrificed her marriage for her career. Dancer Ann Lawrence gave birth after killing her child's father. The mountain climbers find Johnny alive, and while they make the journey back, Phyllis discovers that the boy is Ann's son, but Ann decides that Susan should keep him.

Leif Erickson and Eleanor Parker.

Ruth Roman, Eleanor Parker, and Patricia Neal.

RW:

" I realized *Three Secrets* was soap opera, but I liked the idea. I hadn't done a woman's picture and was intrigued by working with the three actresses who were already cast for it, particularly Patricia Neal. My favorite piece is the rescue effort. To help make it more believable, I was intent on getting every bit of texture in the mountain-climbing area. The mountaineers

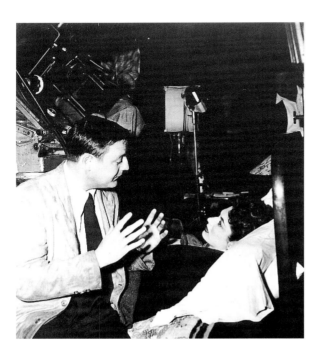

were actual climbers from the Sierra Club, and the interviewer was a real one, Bill Welsh. We had no script set on it, just the general idea of what we wanted to be said. I told Bill, 'You know what you're after. Just hold an interview with these people.' They knew the story, what they were there for, so I didn't give them any lines. What you see on the screen is an actual interview with a TV commentator and real mountain climbers worked into our situation."

Wise and Ruth Roman.

TWO FLAGS WEST
(20th Century-Fox, 1950)

Directed by Robert Wise. Produced by Casey Robinson. Screenplay: Casey Robinson, based on a story by Frank S. Nugent and Curtis Kenyon. Director of Photography: Leon Shamroy. Music: Hugo Friedhofer. Musical Director: Alfred Newman. Orchestration: Earle Hagen, Maurice de Packh. Special Photographic Effects: Fred Sersen. Wardrobe: Charles Le Maire. Art Direction: Lyle Wheeler, Chester Core. Set Decoration: Thomas Little, Fred J. Rode. Makeup Artist: Ben Nye. Sound: Alfred Bruzlin, Harry M. Leonard. Film Editor: Louis Loeffler. Former Title: "Trumpet to the Morn." 92 minutes.

Cast: Joseph Cotten (Colonel Clay Tucker), Linda Darnell (Elena Kenniston), Jeff Chandler (Major Henry Kenniston), Cornel Wilde (Captain Mark Bradford), Dale Robertson (Lem), Jay C. Flippen (Sergeant Terrance Duey), Noah Beery (Cy Davis), Harry Von Zell (Ephraim Strong), John Sands (Lieutenant Adams), Arthur Hunnicutt (Sergeant Pickens), Jack Lee (Courier), Robert Adler (Hank), Harry Carter (Lieutenant Reynolds), Ferris Taylor (Dr. Magowan), Sally Corner (Mrs. Magowan), Everett Glass (Reverend Simpkins), Marjorie Bennett (Mrs. Simpkins), Lee MacGregor (Cal), Roy Gordon (Captain Stanley), Aurora Castillo (Maria), Stanley Andrews (Colonel Hoffman), Don Garner (Ash Cooper).

Joseph Cotten and Jeff Chandler.

A group of Confederate prisoners, led by Colonel Clay Tucker, is granted freedom on the proviso that they serve with a Union outfit and help in the fight against Indians. Captain Mark Bradford escorts them to Fort Thorn, commanded by Major Henry Kenniston, a man bitter at the fact that a physical disability precludes him from taking part in the war. Kenniston harbors a strong passion for his brother's widow, Elena, who is also loved by Bradford. Tucker and his men, who accepted the amnesty so they could escape, begin to plan their break. When the chance presents itself, Kenniston needlessly orders the son of the Kiowa chief killed, and the Southerners decide to return to the fort and aid in the fierce battle that ensues. Bradford is among the casualties, and Kenniston realizes that the Indians will only be pacified if he gives himself up. With Kenniston dead, Tucker is left in charge of the fort, knowing that the war for secession is about to end.

Cornel Wilde, Linda Darnell and Jeff Chandler.

RW:

“ I've always been fascinated by the chemistry between certain people and the camera. It's something you can't go to acting school for. We had a tough location on *Two Flags West*. Very often it was windy and hot. As we were out there shooting, I noticed that Jeff Chandler was always hanging around on his days off. When an actor on location, particularly a rough one, is not called for the day, he'll want to go off. But Jeff was never doing that. Finally, I went up to him one day and asked why he was watching the shoot all the time. He said, 'I just love to watch Joe Cotten. He is such a marvelous technician. I'm studying him and learning so much.' The interesting thing is that when the picture was finished, the one who walked off with it and had that magic for the screen was Chandler. Joe was good as always, but he missed that little special thing that Jeff had.

"I had great respect for Darryl Zanuck—he lived up to his reputation for being a very creative man. He also had a reputation in the industry for being an expert on editing. Having been an editor myself, I said, 'Well, let's see.' I had come from RKO, where we had a number of different production heads and it was a practice of all of them, the first time they saw a movie, to say things like 'Change it;' 'Cut that stuff a little bit;' 'That needs trimming.' When we ran *Two Flags*

West for Zanuck, I expected him to start making comments right away. But nothing, not a sound from him. A couple of times somebody whispered in the back and he shushed them up. He just sat and watched the film. The lights came on, he got one of his big cigars, lit it, and sat there for about five minutes rolling his cigar and puffing it, obviously thinking back through the whole picture. Then he started to talk, going through the entire film with his observations, both good and bad. I was so impressed that the man really observed the film, thought about it, and then came up with his suggestions."

Joseph Cotten and Cornel Wilde.

HOUSE ON TELEGRAPH HILL
(20th Century-Fox, 1951)

Directed by Robert Wise. Produced by Robert Bassler. Screenplay by Elick Moll and Frank Partos, based on the novel "The Frightened Child" by Dana Lyon. Director of Photography: Lucien Ballard. Music: Sol Kaplan. Musical Director: Alfred Newman. Orchestration: Edward B. Powell, Maurice de Packh. Assistant Director: Horace Hough. Costumes: Renie. Wardrobe Supervisor: Charles Le Maire. Special Photographic Effects: Fred Sersen. Art Direction: Lyle Wheeler, John De Cuir. Set Decoration: Thomas Little, Paul S. Fox. Makeup Artist: Ben Nye. Sound: George Leverett, Harry M. Leonard. Film Editor: Nick DeMaggio. 93 minutes.

Cast: Richard Basehart (Alan Spender), Valentina Cortesa (Victoria Kowelska), William Lundigan (Major Marc Anders), Fay Baker (Margaret), Gordon Gebert (Chris), Kei Thing Chung (Houseboy), Steve Geray (Dr. Burkhardt), Herbert Butterfield (Callahan), John Burton (Mr. Whitmore), Mario Siletti (Tony), Charles Wagenheim (Man at Accident), David Clarke (Mechanic), Tamara Schee (Maria), Natasha Lytess (Karin), Ashmead Scott (Inspector Hardy), Mari Young (Chinese Girl Singer), Tom McDonough (Farrell), Henry Rowland (Sergeant-Interpreter), Les O'Pace (UNRRA Sergeant), Don Kohler (Chemist), Harry Carter (Detective Ellis).

Richard Basehart and Valentina Cortesa.

Academy Award nomination for best art direction in black and white.

During World War II, Polish-born Victoria Kowelska is confined to the concentration camp of Belsen, where the horrors of her daily life are somewhat alleviated by her friendship with another inmate, Karin. In the course of their conversations, Karin confides that her son Chris is being cared for by a rich aunt who lives in San Francisco. After Karin dies and the camp is liberated by the American army, Victoria assumes her friend's identity so that she can come to the United States. Upon arriving in New York, she learns that Karin's wealthy aunt has died, leaving her entire fortune to Chris. Victoria marries the boy's guardian, Alan Spender, and moves to the family's mansion atop Telegraph Hill in San Francisco. Her fears that her deception could be discovered are eased when Chris accepts her as his real mother, but Victoria gradually grows suspicious that Alan, helped by Chris's governess, Margaret, is trying to kill her and the boy to gain complete control of the money. In an attempt to poison Victoria, Alan is tricked into poisoning himself and dies. Margaret, who refused to call a doctor when Alan was expiring, is arrested for his murder.

RW:

"When I was handed the script for *House on Telegraph Hill*, I liked the idea of the San Francisco location but thought it was a routine kind of mystery. I told Bob Bassler, the producer, that I didn't want to do it. The next day, I was summoned to Mr. Zanuck's office. He said, 'I understand you don't want to do *House on Telegraph Hill*.' I said, 'That's right. The script is professionally done but there's no new ground there. I just don't have any enthusiasm for it.' And he said, 'Bob, let me tell you something. I've been in this business a long time. If you find one project every two or three years that you're really enthused about, you'll be very lucky in your career. It may not be the greatest story in the world, but I wish you would do it.' I said, 'All right, Darryl, as long as you understand how I feel about it, I'll go in and give it everything I can.' The best thing about it was working with the cast, especially Valentina Cortesa, a lovely woman and a fine actress."

Valentina Cortesa and William Lundigan.

Lock Martin, Patricia Neal, and Michael Rennie.

THE DAY THE EARTH STOOD STILL
(20th Century-Fox, 1951)

Directed by Robert Wise. Produced by Julian Blaustein. Screenplay: Edmund H. North, based on the story "Farewell to the Master" by Harry Bates. Director of Photography: Leo Tover. Music: Bernard Herrmann. Special Photographic Effects: Fred Sersen. Costumes: Travilla. Wardrobe Direction: Charles Le Maire. Klaatu's Costume: Perkins Bailey. Assistant Director: Art Lueker. Art Direction: Lyle Wheeler, Addison Hehr. Set Decoration: Thomas Little, Claude Carpenter. Makeup Artist: Ben Nye. Sound: Arthur L. Kirbach, Harry M. Leonard. Film Editor: William Reynolds. 92 minutes.

Cast: Michael Rennie (Klaatu), Patricia Neal (Helen Benson), Hugh Marlowe (Tom Stevens), Sam Jaffe (Professor Barnhardt), Billy Gray (Bobby Benson), Frances Bavier (Mrs. Barley), Lock Martin (Gort), Drew Pearson (Himself), Carleton Young (Colonel), Frank Conroy (Harley), Fay Roope (Major General), Edith Evanson (Mrs. Crockett), Robert Osterloh (Major White), Tyler McVey (Brady), James Seay (Government Man), John Brown (Mr. Barley), Marjorie Crossland (Hilda), Glenn Hardy (Interviewer), House Peters, Jr. (M.P. Captain), Rush Williams (M.P. Sergeant), Olan Soule (Mr. Kurll), Gil Herman (Government Agent), Gabriel Heater, H. V. Kaltenborn and Elmer Davis (Commentators).

Golden Globe Award for the Best Film Promoting International Understanding.

Michael Rennie.

*Michael Rennie
and Billy Gray.*

*Patricia Neal,
Billy Gray, and
Hugh Marlowe.*

*Billy Gray and
Michael Rennie.*

Wise directs Billy Gray and Michael Rennie.

Lock Martin and Michael Rennie.

Patricia Neal and Lock Martin.

*T*he eyes of the world converge on Washington, D.C. when a flying saucer lands on the capital's mall. From inside the ship emerge an alien of human features, Klaatu, and an eight-foot-tall metallic robot, Gort. As he reaches inside his spacesuit for an object that turns out to be a gift for the president, Klaatu is shot by a soldier. Gort reacts by destroying all weapons in sight before being stopped by Klaatu, who is then taken to a hospital. The alien seeks a meeting with all the leaders of the world but is informed by a member of the White House staff that such a gathering would be unthinkable. Klaatu escapes the hospital and, in order to better understand the people of the Earth, takes a room in a boarding house under the name of Mr. Carpenter, befriending a young widow, Helen Benson, and her son Bobby. Klaatu hits upon the idea of delivering his message to the great minds of the world, and contacts the prominent Professor Barnhardt. In a non-violent demonstration of his powers, the alien stops all electricity on Earth for thirty minutes, but the display only heightens the hostility fomented against him by the government and the media. As he tries to reach his spaceship, where Barnhardt's peers will soon join him, Klaatu is mortally wounded by the military. Acting on his instructions, Helen seeks Gort's help. The robot retrieves Klaatu's body and brings it back to life. Before leaving, Klaatu tells the assembled scientists that other planets have come to enjoy peaceful coexistence because of the vigilance of an army of robots like Gort and that Earth will face obliteration if it carries its belligerent ways into space.

RW:

" One of the challenges was the Gort character himself. We knew we had to have some kind of suit that somebody could be in. This was before we had such a great number of 6'8", 7'2" basketball players, and we were searching all over for a very tall man, going to extra casting people and casting departments. Somebody remembered that the Grauman's Chinese Theater had in those days a terribly tall doorman. He was 7'7" and we hired him to be in that suit. He was not a very strong man, and that suit was heavy. He could only stay in it for about half an hour at a time. He couldn't pick up Pat Neal. For the shot where she falls against the chairs and he's coming toward her, I panned to let him go behind a door, stopped filming and held on the door. With the help of a crane, we picked Pat up, turned him around and put her in his arms. So when we started the camera again, he walked out of the frame with Pat being carried all the way by a wire. Then, on the reverse shot, we put a lightweight dummy in his arms. Just one of the little tricks we had to do to make the robot believable. And we had to have two suits

Lock Martin and Patricia Neal.

This still from the scene in which Patrica Neal is carried by the robot shows the suit with the laces up the front.

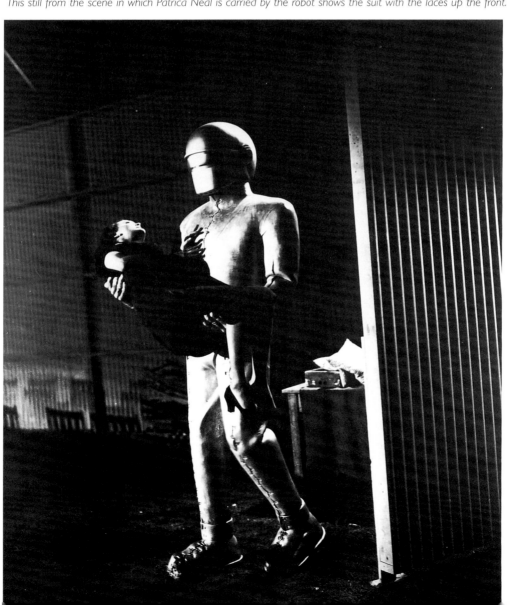

for him. One with a zipper down the back for when he had his front to the camera, another with a zipper up the front for the shots of his back.

"Any script where you're going to need military aid has to get approval of the Department of Defense. They wouldn't give us an okay for the equipment we needed because they didn't like the theme of our picture. We went to the National Guard and had no problems. All the troops and equipment in our shots in Washington are the Washington National Guard's, as opposed to the regular Army. I didn't shoot that stuff; I had a second-unit director. I went back with him and spent a couple of weeks there laying out the shots and planning it all very carefully, so he shot what I wanted. That was done for economic reasons. Of course, I prefer to do all my so-called second unit, but, within the terms of our budget, there was no way I would be able to go back there and shoot that material.

"*The Day the Earth Stood Still* was shot at a time when the impact of television was coming on pretty strong. The box-office was dropping off and the studios were tightening up the budgets. Zanuck had cautioned me a couple of times in memos about shooting too many angles. I shot a sequence around the breakfast table in the boarding house, and I had planned carefully just the angles I needed to make the whole thing go together. Zanuck chose that one to write me a very harsh memo saying, 'I've been warning you about overshooting. I saw yesterday's rushes and you have all these angles around the breakfast table. I think this must stop now. Otherwise, I'm going to take some kind of measure.' I sat down and wrote him a very detailed memo of just what coverage I had and why I felt it was necessary. I never heard another thing from him. He respected how I had laid it out.

"I think many of my films have an importance to them in what they say about man and his condition and the world around him, how he faces it and overcomes it. I always want my films to have a comment to make. However, the comment should be made by the story itself, the development of the plot and the interplay of the characters, without having the actors say it in so many words. *The Day the Earth Stood Still* is an exception to that. The whole purpose of it was for Klaatu to deliver that warning at the end. I feel very strongly in favor of what the movie says. It's very much of a forerunner in its warning about atomic warfare, and it shows that we must all learn to get along together. I liked the fact that it was science-fiction, but science-fiction on Earth, not another trip to the moon, giving us the chance to address some very important issues."

THE CAPTIVE CITY

(United Artists/Aspen, 1952)

Directed by Robert Wise. Produced by Theron Warth. Screenplay by Karl Kamb and Alvin Josephy, Jr. Story: Alvin Josephy, Jr. Director of Photography: Lee Garmes. Photographed with the Hoge Lens. Music composed by Jerome Moross. Musical Director: Emil Newman. Assistant to Director Wise: Ralph Hoge. Assistant Director: Ivan Volkman. Photographic Effects: William Reinhold. Production Designer: Maurice Zuberano. Casting Director: Jack Baur. Sound Supervision: James G. Stewart. Sound: Tom Carmon. Film Editor: Ralph Swink. Former Title: "Tightrope." 91 minutes.

Cast: John Forsythe (Jim Austin), Joan Camden (Marge Austin), Harold J. Kennedy (Don Carey), Marjorie Crossland (Mrs. Sirak), Victor Sutherland (Murray Sirak), Ray Teal (Chief Gillette), Martin Milner (Phil Harding), Geraldine Hall (Mrs. Nelson), Hal K. Dawson (Clyde Nelson), Ian Wolfe (Reverend Nash), Gladys Hurlbut (Linda Percy), Jess Kirkpatrick (Anderson), Paul Newlan (Krug), Frances Morris (Mrs. Harding), Paul Brinegar (Police Sergeant), Patricia Goldwater (Sally Carey), Robert Gorrell (Joe Berg), Glenn Judd (Coverly), William C. Miller (Coroner).

After an all-night drive, Jim Austin, accompanied by his wife, Marge, arrives at a police station in the small town of Warren and informs the sergeant in charge that he is being trailed and needs an escort to reach Washington, D.C., safely. As he waits for the police chief to arrive, Austin tape-records his story. Having settled in Kennington, a typical medium-sized Midwestern city, Austin is quite content with his life as part-owner of a daily newspaper. His perception of this ideal community begins to change when a private detective, Clyde Nelson, tells him how a simple investigation for a divorce settlement case led to Nelson's being harassed by the local police when he uncovered the shady dealings of a real estate broker, Murray Sirak. The journalist is reluctant to accept the truth of the facts until Nelson is killed. Austin's own probing opens his eyes

to a widespread network of organized crime involving the town's most prominent citizens. Pressure is brought to bear—the paper's press privileges are revoked, advertisers pull their ads, threats come from all sides. Still, Austin engages in a one-man crusade to clean Kennington of the criminal element. His options seemingly exhausted, a news report on the Senate Crime Investigation Committee catches his attention and he decides to go to Washington and testify. The police chief of Warren arrives as the journalist finishes his recording, and provides an escort for the Austins.

RW:

“ *The Captive City* was one of the first films made for United Artists under the aegis of Arthur Krim, Robert Benjamin, and Max Youngstein, who had taken it over. We tried for a long time to get it made until UA said they would go for it. We had a $250,000 budget and they would only put $175,000 up, so we had to dig up another $75,000 to complete the finance, which we got through a very wealthy man who dealt with the stock exchange and was interested in movies. We were completely on our own. It was a most stimulating, exciting, and fulfilling period of filmmaking for me. The movie didn't cause any attention here, but I remember getting a review from England that called it 'the sleeper of the year.' I was very proud of it, especially for its documentary-like visual texture. Lee Garmes, a master cinematographer, did an outstanding job using the Hoge Lens and getting marvelous deep-focus effects.

"I knew Bernard Herrmann from *Citizen Kane, All That Money Can Buy,* and *The Magnificent Ambersons.* He was a fine composer, and his early use of electronic scoring in *The Day the Earth Stood Still* was most effective. Bernie was a great talent but very irascible and temperamental. When I was getting wound up on the editing of *The Captive City,* he called me, saying, 'Bob, I'd like to do the score for it.' I said, 'Bernie, we have barely enough money, we can't afford you.' He kept nudging me, but I wouldn't tell him what our budget for scoring

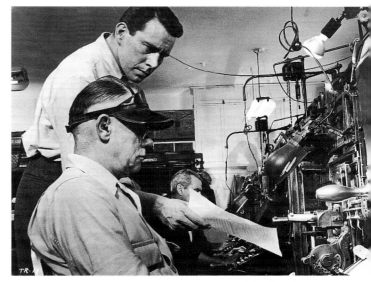

John Forsythe.

was. He wanted to do the film and said, 'Let me see you there.' He came to the studio one day and we were talking when he asked, 'How much money do you have for the music score?' I said, 'Bernie our whole budget on the picture is $250,000. We only have $10,000 for the music.' He stopped and went right through the roof: 'How dare you! That wouldn't be enough for the orchestration, for God's sake!' He ranted and raved, and stormed out of the office. I knew it all the time. I tried to talk him out of it, but he wouldn't listen."

SOMETHING FOR THE BIRDS

(20th Century-Fox, 1952)

Directed by Robert Wise. Produced by Samuel G. Engel. Screenplay by I. A. L. Diamond and Boris Ingster, based on stories by Alvin M. Josephy, Joseph Petracca, and Boris Ingster. Director of Photography: Joseph LaShelle. Music: Sol Kaplan. Musical Director: Lionel Newman. Orchestration: Bernard Mayers. Special Photographic Effects: Ray Kellogg. Art Direction: Lyle Wheeler, George Patrick. Set Decoration: Thomas Little, Bruce MacDonald. Costumes Designed by Elois Jenssen. Wardrobe Direction: Charles Le Maire. Assistant Director: Henry Weinberger. Sound: Arthur L. Kirbach, Harry M. Leonard. Film Editor: Hugh S. Fowler. 81 minutes.

Cast: Victor Mature (Steve Bennett), Patricia Neal (Anne Richards), Edmund Gwenn (Johnny Adams), Larry Keating (Patterson), Gladys Hurlbut (Mrs. Rice), Hugh Sanders (Grady), Christian Rub (Leo), Wilton Graff (Taylor), Walter Baldwin (Bigelow), Archer MacDonald (Lemmer), Richard Garrick (Chandler), Ian Wolfe (Foster), Russell Gaige (Winthrop), Louise Lorimer (Mrs. Winthrop), John Brown (Mr. Lund), Camillo Guercio (Duncan), Joan Miller (Mac), Madge Blake (Mrs. Chadwick), Norman Field (Judge), Sam McDaniel (Chief), Gordon Nelson (O'Malley), Emmett Vogan (Beecham), John Ayres (Congressman Walker), Charles Watts (Jessup), Rodney Bell (Announcer), Norma Varden (Congresswoman Bates), Leo Curley (Congressman Macy), John Maxwell (Congressman Craig).

Patricia Neal and Edmund Gwenn.

Johnny Adams, an employee at a Washington, D.C., printing plant for thirty-six years, every so often pockets one of the many invitations he engraves and, donning a tuxedo, attends the capital's most glittering social events. He is always a popular guest, known among the V.I.P.s as the Admiral. At a reception, Johnny meets Anne Richards, a representative of the Society for the Preservation of the California Condor, who is in Washington to stop Continental Gas from drilling in a condor sanctuary. Anne's efforts to see a prominent member of the government have been in vain, and she asks Johnny for help. Fearful of exposing himself, Johnny refuses at first, but ends up introducing Anne to Steve Bennett, a professional lobbyist. Taking a personal interest in Anne, Steve promises to help, only to discover that his firm represents the gas company. Discouraged, Anne decides to return to California, but Johnny promises to pull some strings. A radio commentator, Patterson, unmasks the bogus Admiral, and Johnny appears before a Senate Investigating Committee on lobbyism, winning the crowd with his account of how he became a party crasher. Behind the scenes, Steve engages several organizations in pressuring Continental Gas to drop its drilling plans. With the bill defeated, Johnny returns to his job and engraves Anne and Steve's wedding invitations.

Christian Rub and Edmund Gwenn.

RW:

❝ Sam Engel was a contract producer at Fox, and he had the script for *Something for the Birds* done a long time before I came on it. When I accepted it, I.A.L. Diamond was brought in to do a rewrite of the earlier drafts, and I worked with him for a few weeks. Diamond was a very good writer, with a biting sense of humor, and he brought a lot of funny scenes and lines into the script. Edmund Gwenn was the reason why they made the film. They were looking for something for him to do after his big success in *Mister 880*. He was a delightful old gentleman to work with. He was well along in his seventies and would rattle a page or two of dialogue with great ease. Overall, I thought *Something for the Birds* was a better film than its fate seemed to decree. That's one Fox film I did not try to get out of.❞

Victor Mature, Edmund Gwenn, and Patricia Neal.

DESTINATION GOBI
(20th Century-Fox, 1953)

Directed by Robert Wise. Produced by Stanley Rubin. Screenplay: Everett Freeman, based on a story by Edmund G. Love. Director of Photography (Technicolor): Charles G. Clarke. Music: Sol Kaplan. Musical Direction: Alfred Newman. Orchestration: Edward B. Powell. Color Consultant: Leonard Doss. Special Photographic Effects: Ray Kellogg. Assistant Director: J. Richard Mayberry. Art Direction: Lyle Wheeler, Lewis Creber. Set Decoration: Al Orenbach. Makeup Artist: Ben Nye. Wardrobe Direction: Charles Le Maire. Sound: Arthur L. Kirbach, Harry M. Leonard. Film Editor: Robert Fritch. Former Title: "Sixty Saddles For Gobi." 89 minutes.

Cast: Richard Widmark (C.P.O. Sam McHale), Don Taylor (Jenkins), Casey Adams (Walter Landers), Murvyn Vye (Kengtu), Darryl Hickman (Wilbur Cohen), Martin Milner (Elwood Halsey), Ross Bagdasarian (Paul Sabatello), Judy Dann (Nura-Salu), Rodolfo Acosta (Tomec), Russell Collins (Commander Hobart Wyatt), Leonard Strong (Wali-Akham), Anthony Earl Numkena (Kengtu's Son), Earl Holliman (Frank Swenson), Edgar Barrier (Yin Tang), Alvy Moore (Aide), Stuart Randall (Captain Briggs), William Forrest (Skipper), Bert Moorhouse (Naval Captain), Jack Raine (Admiral).

*I*n the final stages of World War II, the American Navy sends a team of meteorologists to the Gobi Desert to prepare reports deemed vital in the war against Japan. The group is nominally headed by Lieutenant Commander Hobart Wyatt, but actually run by chief petty officer Sam McHale, a by-the-book Navy veteran, upset at being transplanted to the desert. The Americans' site is soon shared with a tribe of Mongol nomads. Worried with the possibility of a Japanese attack on the outfit, McHale attempts to gain the Mongols as allies by offering their leader, Kengtu, sixty saddles as a good will gesture. When a Japanese air raid destroys the installation, killing Wyatt, the Mongols flee overnight, leaving McHale and his seven men alone. Cut off from aid, McHale's only alternative is to cross 800 miles of desert and

Ross Bagdasarian, Richard Widmark, Darryl Hickman, and Casey Adams.

reach the sea. In the course of the arduous trek, Kengtu and his followers save the Americans from treacherous Chinese camel traders. McHale persuades Kengtu to help him, but the Mongol again betrays him, turning the group over to the Japanese. To their astonishment, the Americans are later freed by Kengtu, who conducts them to safety in Okinawa.

RW:

" *Destination Gobi* was intended more as a comedy than an overly serious drama, trying to tell another part of the war that went on globally. It was my first color film and that, along with working with Dick Widmark, is what I enjoyed about it. We had those big, old three-strip Technicolor cameras, and it wasn't easy dealing with this humongous piece of equipment in the desert. It was a tough picture from a location standpoint. We shot it on the Indian reservation at Nixon, Nevada, fifty miles north of Reno. We were there for several weeks in the summer, then went to Fallon, Nevada, for the sand dunes. We used the local Indians for the Mongols. It's amazing—when we researched the pictures of the actual Mongols, you couldn't tell the difference."

Murvyn Vye and Richard Widmark.

THE DESERT RATS
(20th Century-Fox, 1953)

Directed by Robert Wise. Produced by Robert L. Jacks. Written by Richard Murphy. Director of Photography: Lucien Ballard. Music: Leigh Harline. Musical Director: Alfred Newman. Orchestration: Edward B. Powell. Special Photographic Effects: Ray Kellogg. Assistant Director: J. Richard Mayberry. Art Direction: Lyle Wheeler, Addison Hehr. Set Decoration: Fred J. Rode. Wardrobe Direction: Charles Le Maire. Makeup Artist: Ben Nye. Sound: Alfred Bruzlin, Roger Heman. Film Editor: Barbara McLean. 88 minutes.

Cast: Richard Burton (Captain MacRoberts), Robert Newton (Bartlett), Robert Douglas (General), Torin Thatcher (Barney), Chips Rafferty (Smith), Charles Tingwell (Lieutenant Carstairs), Charles Davis (Pete), Ben Wright (Mick), James Mason (Rommel), James Lilburn (Communications Man), John O'Malley (Riley), Ray Harden (Hugh), John Alderson (Corporal), Richard Peel (Rusty), Michael Pate (Captain Currie), Frank Pulaski (Major O'Rourke), Charles Keane (Sergeant Donaldson), Pat O'Moore (Jim), Trevor Constable (Ginger), Albert Taylor (Jensen), John Wengraf (German Doctor), Arno Frey (Kramm), Alfred Ziesler (Von Helmholtz), Charles Fitzsimmons (Fire Officer).

Academy Award nomination for best story & screenplay.

Chips Rafferty and Richard Burton.

April, 1941. The Libyan seaport town of Tobruk, held by the Australian 9th Division, stands in the way of Field Marshal Erwin Rommel's taking of Suez. The Australian General plans to let German panzer divisions break through the defense line without resistance and then close in on the enemy. Captain Tammy MacRoberts, an English career officer, is put in charge of a newly arrived group of untried Australian troopers. Among them is Tom Bartlett, a middle-aged alcoholic whom MacRoberts recognizes as his old schoolmaster. The Captain is a harsh disciplinarian, whose methods irk his men, but Bartlett gets to see his human side as one turns to the other for support. The General's plan is carried out and

MacRoberts participates in several attacks against the Germans. When a vital underground ammunition dump is located, he leads the raiding party that blows it up, but ends up being taken prisoner. At a hospital tent, MacRoberts is face to face with Rommel himself, and the two engage in a verbal confrontation. An allied attack gives the Captain a chance to return to his own lines. The Division makes a last desperate charge against the Germans and Tobruk is saved after 242 days of siege.

James Mason.

The African desert recreated in California.

James Mason.

RW:

" I like *The Desert Rats.* By and large, making it was a very good experience, and it would be a close second to *The Day the Earth Stood Still* as my favorite in the Fox period. I think the scenes of combat are very true. We shot it all in Borrego Springs, out in the desert, not too far from Palm Springs. I researched a lot, running films of the war in the African desert, studying photographs, striving as much as I could to make it look real. That was Richard Burton's second film in this country, after Fox had signed him for the Olivia De Havilland film *My Cousin Rachel.* He was superb, very professional. One of those actors who, if you ask him to make a move in a scene to accommodate the camera, doesn't ask, 'Why? What is my motivation?' He'd just do it."

SO BIG

(Warner Bros., 1953)

Directed by Robert Wise. Produced by Henry Blanke. Screenplay: John Twist, based on the novel by Edna Ferber. Director of Photography: Ellsworth Fredericks. Music: Max Steiner. Orchestrations: Murray K. Cutter. Dialogue Director: Anthony Jowitt. Assistant Director: Russ Saunders. Art Direction: John Beckman. Set Decoration: George James Hopkins. Wardrobe: Milo Anderson, Howard Shoupe. Makeup Artist: Gordon Bau. Sound: Oliver S. Garretson. Film Editor: Thomas Reilly. 101 minutes.

Cast: Jane Wyman (Selina DeJong), Sterling Hayden (Pervus DeJong), Nancy Olson (Dallas O'Mara), Steve Forrest (Dirk DeJong), Elisabeth Fraser (Julie Hempel), Martha Hyer (Paula Hempel), Walter Coy (Roelf Pool), Richard Beymer (Roelf Pool, age 12-16), Tommy Rettig (Dirk DeJong, age 8), Roland Winters (Klaas Pool), Jacques Aubuchon (August Hempel), Ruth Swanson (Maartje Pool), Dorothy Christy (Widow Paarlenberg), Oliver Blake (Adam Coms), Lily Kemble Cooper (Miss Fister), Noralee Norman (Geertje Pool), Jill Janssen (Jozina Pool), Kerry Donnelly (Paula Hempel, age 8), Kenneth Osmond (Eugene, age 9), Lotte Stein (Meena), Arthur Fox (Dirk, age 3), Vera Miles, Evan Loew, Frances Osborne, Jean Garvin, and Carol Grei (Girls), Grandon Rhodes (Bainbridge), Anthony Jochim (Accountant), Herb Vigran (Boss), John Maxwell (Reverend Dekker), Bud Osborne (Wagon Driver), Ray Bennett (Al).

Sterling Hayden, Arthur Fox, and Jane Wyman.

Selina Peak, a student at an exclusive private school, learns that her gambler father died penniless. She sells all her belongings, pays her father's debts, and takes the post of schoolteacher in a Dutch farm community on the outskirts of Chicago. She lodges with the Pool family, taking a special interest in young Roelf Pool, encouraging him to pursue a musical career. At a social gathering, Selina meets Pervus DeJong, a poor truck farmer

*Tommy Rettig and
Jane Wyman.*

*Jane Wyman and
Richard Beymer.*

*Steve Forrest,
Jane Wyman,
Walter Coy, and
Nancy Olson.*

Jane Wyman and Sterling Hayden.

Jane Wyman and Steve Forrest.

who tells her he is always being cheated at the market. Selina offers to teach him arithmetic and, as time passes, they grow fond of each other and marry. The years of hardship that follow are brightened by the birth of Dirk, the son she calls So Big. When Dirk is eight years old, Pervus dies of pneumonia and Selina takes the reins of the farm, gradually turning it into a profitable enterprise that pays for her son's education. Selina's dream that Dirk will be a creator of beautiful things seems to come true when he graduates as an architect, but Dirk soon bypasses the drawing board for a more lucrative position as a sales executive. Disappointed, Selina gets consolation from Roelf Pool's success as a concert pianist. Having fallen in love with Dallas O'Mara, a painter who values artistic integrity over financial reward, Dirk, on a visit to the farm with Dallas and Roelf, tells Selina he will dedicate himself to architecture.

RW:

" Generally, I had quite good relationships with producers before I became an independent. Most of the time they left me alone making my film. I never had any of my producers trying to take over or use a very strong hand with me. Because I had been an editor and got off to a good start working with Val Lewton at RKO, I think they had respect for me as somebody who knew my way around finishing up films after they were shot, so I was involved with my pictures pretty much all the way through. On *So Big* I worked with Henry Blanke, a very nice gentleman and a creative producer. He had been at Warners for twenty years and still had several more to go in a long contract. They were trying in every way they could to put pressure on him—demean him in a way—hoping somehow to make him say, 'The heck with it, cancel my contract and let me out.' They really seemed determined to make him get disgusted, but he stayed on until 1961."

EXECUTIVE SUITE
(Metro-Goldwyn-Mayer, 1954)

Directed by Robert Wise. Produced by John Houseman. Associate Producer: Jud Kinberg. Screenplay by Ernest Lehman, based on the novel by Cameron Hawley. Director of Photography: George J. Folsey. Special Effects: A. Arnold Gillespie, Warren Newcombe. Women's Costumes Designed by Helen Rose. Art Direction: Cedric Gibbons, Edward Carfagno. Set Decoration: Edwin B. Willis, Emile Kuri. Assistant Director: George Rhein. Makeup Artist: William Tuttle. Hair Styles: Sydney Guilaroff. Recording Supervisor: Douglas Shearer. Film Editor: Ralph E. Winters. 104 minutes.

Cast: William Holden (McDonald Walling), June Allyson (Mary Blemond Walling), Barbara Stanwyck (Julia O. Tredway), Fredric March (Loren Phineas Shaw), Walter Pidgeon (Frederick Y. Alderson), Shelley Winters (Eva Bardeman), Paul Douglas (Josiah Walter Dudley), Louis Calhern (George Nyle Caswell), Dean Jagger (Jesse Q. Grimm), Nina Foch (Erica Martin), Tim Considine (Mike Walling), William Phipps (Bill Lundeen), Lucille Knoch (Mrs. George Nyle Caswell), Mary Adams (Sara Asenath Grimm), Virginia Brissac (Edith Alderson), Edgar Stehli (Julius Steigel), Harry Shannon (Ed Benedeck), Charles Wagenheim (Luigi Cassoni), Virginia Filer (Western Union Operator), Jonathan Cott (Cop), Robin Camp (Mailroom Boy), Ray Mansfield (Alderson Secretary), A. Cameron Grant and Bert Davidson (Salesmen), May McAvoy (Grimm Secretary), Willis Bouchey and John Doucette (Morgue Officials), Esther Michelson and Gus Schilling (News Dealers), Abe Dinovitch (Cab Driver), Faith Geer (Stork Club Hat Check Girl), Mimi Doyle (Telephone Operator), Mary Alan Hokanson (Nurse), Paul Bryar (Stork Club Waiter), John Banner (Enrique), Roy Engel (Jimmy Farrell), Madie Norman (Walling Housekeeper), Dan Riss (City Editor), David McMahon and Ralph Montgomery (Reporters), Raoul Freeman (Avery Bullard), Ann Tyrell (Shaw Secretary).

Academy Award nominations for best supporting actress (Nina Foch), cinematography in black and white, art direction in black and white, and costume design in black and white. Special Jury Prize for ensemble acting at the Venice Film Festival. National Board of Review Award for best supporting actress (Foch).

*Louis Calhern,
Paul Douglas,
Fredric March,
Barbara Stanwyck,
William Holden,
and Nina Foch.*

Fredric March and Nina Foch.

Walter Pidgeon, Nina Foch, Dean Jagger, Louis Calhern, Shelley Winters, Fredric March, Barbara Stanwyck, William Holden, June Allyson, and Paul Douglas.

Fredric March, Paul Douglas, and Shelley Winters.

President of Tredway Corporation, the country's third-largest manufacturer of furniture, Avery Bullard sends a telegram from New York to the company's headquarters in Pennsylvania calling for an executive board meeting. As he tries to catch a taxi, he has a stroke and dies. Bullard ran Tredway as a one-man company, without ever naming an executive vice-president. With his post vacant, five men have equal chances of replacing him—Frederick Alderson, senior officer; Loren Shaw, vice-president and comptroller; Josiah Dudley, vice-president in charge of sales; Jesse Q. Grimm, vice-president in charge of manufacturing; and McDonald Walling, vice-president in charge of design. Ambitious and calculating, Shaw moves quickly to fill the vacuum created by Bullard's death, arranging a meeting for the following day to have the new president elected. Four votes will give him the post, and, by means of coercion, he secures the support of Dudley and corrupt stock manipulator George Nyle Caswell. The seventh member of the board, Julia Tredway, daughter of the corporation's founder and its major stockholder, is talked by Shaw into supporting him. Resigned to being a second in command, Alderson will not challenge Shaw; Grimm had already made up his mind to leave the company. So it is up to

*Studio head Dore Schary and Barbara Stanwyck on the set of **Executive Suite**.*

Walling to oppose the comptroller, a man he believes has sacrificed the company's tradition of quality product to achieve larger profits. In the meeting, Walling makes an impassioned speech and is chosen the new president.

16-Jox-42

William Holden and Wise.

RW:

❝ When we got to the climactic boardroom sequence, we stopped
for a day. I went into the set with the cast and the cameraman,
George Folsey, and played the whole sequence so that we could study
it in terms of how we wanted to treat it. We worked it up and broke
the scenes down, so we had a feeling of the tempo and the performances. We made still pictures, little diagrams, and notes on how we
were going to cover. When we finally got it all worked out, we just
went in the next day and started shooting it. By planning like that, you
can save yourself a lot of time because while you're shooting in one
direction, you can pretty well go through the sequence and keep
getting your shots in that one direction before you turn around and get
your reverses, when you have to change all your lighting again. That
allowed us to shoot the whole sequence in less time than we would
had we not had the rehearsal and had to go cutting piece by piece.

"I had a wonderful group of actors. Up until the boardroom, I
guess I didn't have them all together in the same room. They were a
lot of fun because most of them had worked together over the years.

They used to kid each other, joke, and tell stories. They'd be sitting around while the lighting was being finished, swapping yarns and needling each other; but the minute the bell rang, playtime was off and they went right back into character.

"I had a very interesting experience with Fredric March. He had appeared in Stanley Kramer's film of *Death of a Salesman* and got criticized by the reviewers who thought his performance had been overboard. This concerned me a lot because the part Freddie was to play in *Executive Suite* was a very rich one. He was always twitching and nervous, wiping his hands off with a handkerchief. I thought that if Freddie tried to overdo the part, it was going to be too much, but I didn't know how to approach him about this. I'd been shooting for a couple of weeks when he reported for work. I knew I had to face him with the interpretation of his character. He said to me, 'When I first read the script, I thought of all the special business I can do with it.' My heart sank. Then he said, 'When I read it again, I started thinking that maybe the less I do, the better for this character.' I said, 'That's exactly how I feel!' He said, 'I'm glad you agree, but you know I'm an actor—we can all tend to ham it up. If I start to get a little too broad, just come up and whisper in my ear, and I'll tone it down.' He got too rich only two or three times during the filming, and I just went up and said, 'Freddie, it's building. Bring it down.' He thanked me and immediately brought his performance in line.

"Many years ago, in the early days of sound films, when underscoring was a little younger, people would ask, 'Why do you need music in that sequence?' When thinking about the scores for my films, I ask myself a different question—'What can music do in this sequence to bring out what I want it to say?' A good score, when used in the right way, can add qualities and dimensions that enrich and strengthen your film. A very important aspect of choosing where to have music in a film is where you don't use it, for as valuable as where the music should go is where there shouldn't be any. In rare instances, a whole film can do without an underscoring. In *The Set-Up*, the only pieces of music come from jukeboxes on the street. In *Executive Suite* there's no music at all. At the time of *Executive Suite*, Dore Schary was the head of production at MGM, and it was one of his favorite projects. We all had a meeting one day, and, as we were talking about the various facets of it, he said, 'I think it will be most effective just not to have any score at all in this film.' We agreed to try it. If it didn't work for the film, we could always add a score later. But we all liked it when we saw the finished film."

HELEN OF TROY
(Warner Bros., 1955)

Directed by Robert Wise. Screenplay by John Twist and Hugh Gray, based on Homer's "Iliad." Adaptation: Hugh Gray and N. Richard Nash. Director of Photography (Warnercolor, CinemaScope): Harry Stradling. Music: Max Steiner. Orchestrations: Murray Cutter. Second-Unit Director: Yakima Canutt (and, uncredited, Raoul Walsh). Second-Unit Photographers: Sid Hickox, Amerigo Gengarelli. Special Photographic Effects: Louis Lichtenfield. Assistant Director: Gus Agosti. Continuity Sketches: Maurice Zuberano. Art Direction: Edward Carrere. Assistant Art Director: Ken Adam. Costumes Designed by Roger Furse. Production Managers: Maurizo Lodi-Fe, Giuseppi De Blasio. Bacchanal Choreography: Madi Obolensky. Makeup Supervisor: Gordon Bau. Makeup Artist: Bill Phillips. Hair Stylist: Alfred Scott. Sound: Charles Lang. Film Editor: Thomas Reilly. 118 minutes.

   Cast: Rossana Podesta (Helen), Jack Sernas (Paris), Sir Cedric Hardwicke (Priam), Stanley Baker (Achilles), Niall MacGinnis (Menelaus), Nora Swinburne (Hecuba), Robert Douglas (Agamemnon), Torin Thatcher (Ulysses), Harry Andrews (Hector), Janette Scott (Cassandra), Ronald Lewis (Aeneas), Brigitte Bardot (Andraste), Eduardo Ciannelli (Andros), Marc Lawrence (Diomedes), Maxwell Reed (Ajax), Robert Brown (Polydorus), Barbara Cavan (Cora), Terence Longdon (Patroclus), Patricia Marmont (Andromache), Guido Notari (Nestor), Tonio Selwart (Adelphous), Georges Zoritch (Dance Specialty), Esmond Knight (The High Priest).

*I*n the year 1100 B.C., King Priam, monarch of the prosperous city of Troy, sends his son Paris on a mission of peace to avoid war with the Greek kingdoms. In the midst of a storm, Paris is swept out to sea, being later found on the coast of Sparta by Queen Helen. Struck by Helen's beauty, and believing she is a slave of King Menelaus, Paris falls in love with her. His health regained, he arrives at the Spartan palace, interrupting a council meeting of the Greek kings. To prove his identity, Paris fights the powerful Ajax. Helen's emotional reaction to the match convinces Menelaus that she knows the Trojan prince, and he has Paris imprisoned. With the help of trusted slaves, Helen frees Paris, and as they say good-bye, Greek soldiers arrive. Paris and Helen dive

Rossana Podesta and Jack Sernas.

into the ocean and are taken to a Phoenician boat, which carries them safely to Troy. The initial jubilation over the prince's return turns to resentment when Helen's identity is revealed and King Priam recognizes that a devastating war will be inevitable. A thousand Greek ships descend on Troy's shores, and the city's ten-year siege begins. Knowing she is the cause of the conflict, Helen surrenders to her husband, but the Greeks are not satisfied and also demand the riches of Troy. Paris snatches Helen away from Menelaus, returning to the walled city of Troy. The invincible Greek leader Achilles challenges Paris's brother Hector to a personal combat, killing the Trojan. Dozens of arrows are shot at Achilles, but it is Paris who hits his only vulnerable point, the heel. The death of their demi-god demoralizes the Greeks. Before they sail back home, Ulysses explains that he had a gigantic wooden horse built, which he will fill with warriors and leave as a "present" to the Trojans. The Greek ships sail away and King Priam allows his subjects to bring the horse inside the city. When the all-night celebration quiets down, the warriors exit the horse, opening the gates of Troy to the Greek armies. Paris and Helen try to flee, but he is killed by a Spartan soldier. Helen is taken back to Sparta by Menelaus.

Wise instructs the actors at the Cinecitta Studios.

Wise observes Brigitte Bardot and her dialogue coaches.

RW:

““ *Helen of Troy* was an experiment of mine. Color was coming into wide use, CinemaScope had come in, and I felt that it was probably time to get myself into that mainstream of big-size picture-making. It was not that I was mad

Utilizing the full width of the CinemaScope screen creatively was one of Wise's chief concerns when making **Helen of Troy***. Jack Sernas and Rossana Podesta.*

about the material, but I felt it was a challenge and I wanted to see if I could do it successfully. Besides, I was intrigued with the idea of being in Rome and working there. We took about thirty-five crew members from Warners and filled in the rest with local technicians. It's so interesting when you work abroad because film is a common language, not only what we sample on the screen but also among the people who make them. I had my camera, grip, lighting, and special-effects people all from Hollywood, but each one had their own people added from the Italian categories. After two or three days, it was just like being home. They got to know each other and understand the equipment language. It was very interesting to see.

"It had been rather accepted that you couldn't do a lot of cutting with CinemaScope. The whole concept was that you were able to do more comprehensive shots in the wide screen and wouldn't need as many angles as were necessary with the smaller frame. This was nonsense. I saw no reason why I couldn't compose and shoot CinemaScope and edit it just the same way as I had done in the old frame. I decided I could use over-the-shoulder shots, big-head closeups and cut them in as long as I composed them carefully, because you have to balance the closeup with something interesting on the other side. I deliberately tried this in tests and found out there was no reason why I couldn't get the same kind of angles and coverage that I used to get. The only problem with CinemaScope, or any of the anamorphic processes, is that there's no depth of field. That's what I had problems with most of the time in terms of some kinds of shots I'd like to get. I think I was the first one to use editing in its purest sense with CinemaScope."

Jack Sernas, Rossana Podesta, Nora Swinburne and Sir Cedric Hardwicke.

Wrap party for
Helen of Troy.

TRIBUTE TO A BAD MAN

(Metro-Goldwyn-Mayer, 1956)

Directed by Robert Wise. Produced by Sam Zimbalist. Screenplay: Michael Blankfort, based on a story by Jack Schaefer. Director of Photography (Eastmancolor, CinemaScope): Robert Surtees. Music: Miklos Rozsa. Costumes for Irene Papas: Walter Plunkett. Color Consultant: Charles K. Hagedon. Art Direction: Cedric Gibbons, Paul Groesse. Set Decoration: Edwin B. Willis, Fred MacLean. Makeup Artist: William Tuttle. Hair Styles: Sydney Guilaroff. Recording Supervisor: Dr. Wesley C. Miller. Film Editor: Ralph E. Winters. Former Title: "Jeremy Rodock." 95 minutes.

Cast: James Cagney (Jeremy Rodock), Don Dubbins (Steve Miller), Stephen McNally (McNulty), Irene Papas (Jocasta Constantine), Vic Morrow (Lars Peterson), James Griffith (Barjak), Onslow Stevens (Hearn), James Bell (L. A. Peterson), Jeanette Nolan (Mrs. L. A. Peterson), Chubby Johnson (Baldy), Royal Dano (Abe), Lee Van Cleef (Fat Jones), Peter Chong (Cooky).

Wyoming, 1873. As he rides through a valley, Steve Miller, a young Easterner traveling West, comes to the rescue of Jeremy Rodock, a rancher being ambushed by thieves he caught stealing his horses. Af-

Irene Papas and James Cagney.

ter helping him fend off the thieves, Steve removes a bullet from Rodock's body. In gratitude, Rodock offers Steve a job as a hired hand. On the ranch, Steve makes the acquaintance of Jocasta, a young woman whose genuine affection for Rodock is hampered by what she calls his 'hanging fever.' Whenever his vast domains are threatened, Rodock will relentlessly pursue the offenders and dispense his own brand of justice, without any regard for the law. Steve gets a firsthand sample of his employer's blind rage when Rodock summarily executes a horse thief. Later, Rodock catches a foreman he had fired,

Royal Dano, Don Dubbins, and James Cagney.

Lee Van Cleef, James McCallion, Chubby Johnson, Don Dubbins, James Cagney, Royal Dano, and Onslow Stevens.

Irene Papas and James Cagney.

McNulty, and Lars, the rebellious son of his former partner, maiming a number of his horses. His retaliation is to force them to march a long distance barefoot. Disgusted with Rodock's cruelty, Steve decides to leave the ranch and convinces Jocasta, with whom he has fallen in love, to join him. Rodock makes no attempt to stop them, but follows their wagon to give Jocasta a pair of earrings she left behind. Jocasta realizes that Rodock is willing to let his humane, tender side surface and returns to the ranch with him while Steve rides away.

RW:

      I thought the screenplay had an interesting premise, and the idea of directing Spencer Tracy attracted me. The producer, Sam Zimbalist, arranged for me to meet the writer, Michael Blankfort, and Tracy. We had the idea of getting high up in the mountain scene and have lovely green meadows, lakes, and mountains all around as the setting for it. We thought that would be a good change in the background for a western. Tracy called me the next day and asked, 'Bob, do you think we're really right about that? Do you think it's going to be good for me?' He was getting all kinds of second thoughts about it, so I found myself having to buck up his enthusiasm for it. That was my first inkling into the insecurity that man had in many areas. We went ahead, finished the script, and I spent a lot of time down in Colorado, finding a lovely mountain area near Montrose, on the western side of the Rockies, way up high at about 8,5000 feet, with great snowcapped mountains that had never been in pictures.

"In that original meeting, there was also talk about using a new young actress. Irene Papas was suggested and Tracy was very keen on her. As we were approaching the date of shooting, he had a little growth on his face. He was very much of a hypochondriac and he was afraid it might turn out to be malignant. He wanted to have a little surgery on it before we began the picture. He wasn't going to be ready on our starting date, but we were

Tension in the Rockies: Spencer Tracy, assistant director Arvid Griffin and Wise.

locked in to other commitments and went up with the whole troupe to the location. We had scheduled about two weeks' work that we didn't need Tracy for, and I shot a lot of scenes with the juvenile lead, which was being played by a rising young actor, Robert Francis, and Irene Papas. Finally, I ran out of scenes I could shoot with those two and had to go into cover sets, shooting all the scenes in the bunkhouse with the cowboys for a week.

"Just about that time Tracy came up. We arranged our shooting up at the ranch in a way that he could come up for only an hour or two for the first couple of days to get acclimated because it was much higher than the town we were staying in. After that, I still took it very easy—just two or three hours a day. He was being a little irascible with both Bob Francis and Irene Papas, but I attributed that to the altitude. He kept complaining about shortness of breath and suggesting that we move the location to a lower altitude. Finally, about the fifth day, he had a bit of action where he had to bend over and pick up a horse's hoof and examine it. When he came up, he kind of gasped and said, 'Bob, you better get somebody else to replace me. The only way I can finish this film is if you scrub this location and we go down to a lower place.' I just about had it up to my eyeballs by that

James Cagney and Wise.

time. I said, 'Okay, Spencer, we go down the hill and talk to the studio.' I called Sam Zimbalist, who knew of the problems I was having, and told him I couldn't continue with Tracy. An hour later he called me back and said that Tracy was out of the picture.

"I didn't realize it, but people told me later that Tracy had never made a picture for MGM or on loan-out, that a week before he started he didn't ask to be taken out. He was an extremely insecure actor and needed constant reassurance.

But this was the first time they actually pulled the rug from under him. I went over to see him. I was so angry at this man because of the mess he caused, but he was so emotional about it. He was finished now, that was the end of his career. He went into a whole big scene, almost crying. After one hour of this, as mad as I was, I was also feeling sympathy and sorrow for him. Tracy always came on the screen like the Rock of Gibraltar, yet he was actually the reverse of his screen image.

"After a few days waiting, I got a call from Zimbalist saying that James Cagney had agreed to do it but wouldn't be available for a couple of months. There was nothing for us to do but fold everything up and return to Los Angeles. Then misfortune dogged us. During the layoff period, Bob Francis was killed in a plane crash. All the film I shot with him was now no good. We returned to the location and I shot around Cagney for about two weeks. Then Cagney came up and we went ahead with the film. He couldn't have been any more different in terms of his attitude than Tracy. Very professional, very cooperative. He was about the same age as Tracy, but nothing was too rough for him. He took Don Dubbins, who was cast in the Bob Francis role, under his wing and was very helpful to Irene Papas. A complete reverse approach to the part, the picture, and the people he worked with."

SOMEBODY UP THERE LIKES ME
(Metro-Goldwyn-Mayer, 1956)

Directed by Robert Wise. Produced by Charles Schnee. Associate Producer: James E. Newcom. Screenplay by Ernest Lehman, based on the autobiography of Rocky Graziano, written with Rowland Barber. Director of Photography: Joseph Ruttenberg. Music: Bronislau Kaper. Title-song: music by Bronislau Kaper, lyrics by Sammy Cahn, sung by Perry Como. Special Effects: Warren Newcombe. Assistant Director: Robert Saunders. Technical Adviser: Johnny Indrisano. Art Direction: Cedric Gibbons, Malcolm Brown. Set Decoration: Edwin B. Willis, Keogh Gleason. Makeup: William Tuttle. Recording Supervisor: Dr. Wesley C. Miller. Film Editor: Albert Akst. 114 minutes.

Cast: Paul Newman (Rocky Graziano), Pier Angeli (Norma), Everett Sloane (Irving Cohen), Eileen Heckart (Ma Barbella), Sal Mineo (Romolo), Harold J. Stone (Nick Barbella), Joseph Buloff (Benny), Sammy White (Whitney Bimstein), Arch Johnson (Heldon), Robert Lieb (Questioner), Theodore Newton (Commissioner Eagan), Steve McQueen (Fidel), Robert Easton (Corporal), Ray Walker (Ring Announcer), Billy Nelson (Commissioner), Robert Loggia (Frankie Peppo), Matt Crowley (Lou Stillman), Judson Pratt (Johnny Hyland), Donna Jo Gribble (Yolanda Barbella), James Todd (Colonel), Jack Kelk (George), Russ Conway (Captain Grifton), Harry Wismen (Himself), Courtland Shepard (Tony Zale), Sam Taub (Radio Announcer), Terry Rangno (Rocky, age 8), Jan Gillum (Yolanda, age 12), Ralph Vitti (Shorty), Walter Cartier (Polack), John Eldredge (Warden Niles), Clancy Cooper (Captain Lancheck), Dean Jones (Private), Ray Stricklyn (Bryson), Caswell Adams (Sam), Charles Green (Curtis Hightower), Angela Cartwright (Audrey), David Leonard (Mr. Mueller).

Academy Award winner for best cinematography in black and white and art direction in black and white. Academy Award nomination for best editing.

Pier Angeli and Paul Newman.

A street fighter and petty thief, young Rocco Barbella is a typical product of the poor tenements of New York's Lower East Side. Reform school and the penitentiary fail to rein in his aggressive nature. From prison he enters the Army, where he immediately clashes with military discipline, strikes an officer, and runs away. On the lam, he makes some money as a boxer in amateur bouts. Caught by the military police, Rocco is sentenced to a year in Leavenworth Prison, to be followed by dishonorable discharge. In prison, his fistic ability is noted and then honed by a trainer. On discharge, he returns to Stillman's Gym, gets a manager, Irving Cohen, and a trainer, Whitney Bimstein, and adopts the ring name of Rocky Graziano. Several straight knockouts herald the arrival of a new boxing sensation. With his wife, Norma, giving him the love and understanding he never knew before, Rocky works his way up to a title match with the middleweight champion, Tony Zale. Before the fight, a former cellmate, Frankie Peppo, threatens Rocky with telling the press about his prison and Army record if Rocky doesn't throw a warm-up fight. To avoid it, Rocky feigns illness and leaves town. On his return, he is questioned by the District Attorney, refuses to name names, and has his license revoked in New York. The title match is set for Chicago. The night before the fight, Rocky flies to New York, visits his old haunts, and realizes that boxing has saved him from a sordid life. The next day he wins the title.

Paul Newman and Robert Loggia.

Paul Newman.

Paul Newman, Pier Angeli, and Joseph Buloff.

Paul Newman and Everett Sloane.

Wise, Paul Newman, and Pier Angeli.

RW:

    I wanted *Somebody Up There Likes Me* to move around and go like it had a staccato feeling to it. That was like Rocky himself, who was always jiggling around, shuffling his head, twitching a bit—a very nervous kind of guy. I wanted the film to have a little bit of that. Before you start on any film, you have your script timed. There are specialists in that, usually former script supervisors, who take your script, go through it, and time each scene so that you can have a rough idea of how long the film is going to be. Normally, I watch that when shooting and try to keep relatively close to the timing. In this one I made a vow in the beginning to try and bring it ten percent under the timing, whatever it was. I would go in and tell the actors, 'See if you can pick up the cues a little bit. Make it a little faster. Don't worry, it'll work.' I kept pushing, pushing, pushing. You can't just make it an arbitrary thing. Some scenes wouldn't go ten percent under the timing, some probably went a little over, but, by and large, that gave the film a particular bit of energy and drive.

    "Tony Zale, the man Rocky fought the three big fights with, was still very much alive and in excellent shape. Somebody told me, 'Zale, who is strong as an ox, has kept himself in very good shape and works for the Catholic Youth Organization in Chicago

Paul Newman and Eileen Heckart.

Paul Newman and Pier Angeli.

teaching kids to fight. Maybe he can play himself.' I was in New York and came back through Chicago to meet him. He looked great and we made a deal for him to play himself in the film. I thought we were all set on that until we were starting to shoot and Paul Newman was rehearsing with Johnny Indrisano and Tony Zale. After a few days, one of my assistants came to me and said, 'I think you better stop by the rehearsal this evening when you finish. I feel a little uneasy thing about how it's going.' I went down and I could see that Paul was ducking away from the blows. Paul was athletic but had never boxed and he subconsciously was concerned that if, by any chance, one of his blows happened to clip Zale, Tony in reflex would knock him out. That's what a fighter does, without thinking. I recognized it early on, we talked it over and just decided there was no way Paul was going to be able to do it. Fortunately for us, somebody came up with a fighter who just did fighting semi-professionally in small clubs around town and looked almost exactly like Zale.

"MGM had Lower East Side streets in the backlot that were good, but I always felt that it's not a hundred percent believable to shoot even the best exterior set in daylight; it doesn't have quite the same texture. I never buy those beautifully done sets in broad daylight. It works fine at night because you light just what you want to see; it's not as exposed. I insisted with the studio that for all the daytime scenes I needed to go back to New York and shoot in the actual places. I would be happy to shoot all the night exteriors, which were considerable, on the sets back here. In New York, we had to dress the street for a couple of blocks like it would have been twenty years before. We were there for ten days. I needed some local kids, and Steve McQueen was one who came to the office where I was interviewing candidates. There was something about his whole quality that appealed to me and I chose him. With him, I got into a situation where I had to bring him out to the studio to finish a sequence here. We shot it in a day, and I didn't see Steve again until a year later on the set of *This Could Be the Night*, where I was directing his future wife, Neile Adams.

Pier Angeli, Wise, and Everett Sloane.

"We made a thorough and exhaustive examination of the real Rocky. Paul and I spent a lot of time with him in New York so that Paul could study him. We decided that whatever of Graziano's speech patterns, physical movements, and attributes that Paul could make honest for himself, he would try and use, but anything that he felt forced with he would drop. We visited Rocky's haunts, met some of his friends, and got a lot of pictures of him over the years. We were also able to get hold of some tapes done by the author of a *Look* magazine article on Rocky so that Paul could learn how he spoke. In the end, Paul came up with a marvelous performance, as did the whole cast. I was very pleased with Pier Angeli. She was certainly not our idea at the beginning because Rocky's wife, Norma, was American, a New York girl. We were looking for somebody to play her that would be right, but we just couldn't get anybody we seemed to be happy with. At the studio they said, 'We got this young lady here and she's the right age. Sure she's Italian, but we think she's awfully good.' At first I resisted it, but I couldn't come up with someone I liked myself. We tested her and she went into the film. I think it's one of her best performances. There's a lot of strength and femininity in it."

THIS COULD BE THE NIGHT

(Metro-Goldwyn-Mayer, 1957)

Directed by Robert Wise. Produced by Joe Pasternak. Screenplay by Isobel Lennart, based on stories by Cordelia Baird Gross. Director of Photography (CinemaScope): Russell Harlan. Musical Supervision and song "Hustlin' Newsgal" by George Stoll. Title-song: music by Nicholas Brodszky, lyrics by Sammy Cahn. Orchestrations: Billy May, Skip Martin, Robert Van Eps, Don Simpson. Vocal Supervision: Robert Tucker. Music Coordinator: Irving Aaronson. Musical Numbers Staged by Jack Baker. Special Effects: Lee LeBlanc. Assistant Director: Ridgeway Callow. Art Direction: William A. Horning, Paul Groesse. Set Decoration: Edwin B. Willis, Robert R. Benton. Hair Styles: Sydney Guilaroff. Makeup: William Tuttle. Recording Supervisor: Dr. Wesley C. Miller. Film Editor: George Boemler. Other Songs: "I'm Gonna Live Till I Die," by Al Hoffman, Walter Kent and Mann Curtis; "Taking a Chance on Love," by Vernon Duke, John Latouche and Ted Fetter; "Now, Baby, Now," by Nicholas Brodszky and Sammy Cahn; "Sadie Green (The Vamp of New Orleans)," by Gilbert Wells and Johnny Dunn; "I've Got it Bad (And That Ain't Good)," by Duke Ellington and Paul Francis Webster. Former Title: "Protection For a Tough Racket." 103 minutes.

Cast: Jean Simmons (Anne Leeds), Paul Douglas (Rocco), Anthony Franciosa (Tony Armotti), Julie Wilson (Ivy Corlane), Joan Blondell (Crystal), Neile Adams (Patsy St. Clair), J. Carrol Naish (Leon), Rafael Campos (Hussein Mohammed), ZaSu Pitts (Mrs. Shea), Tom Helmore (Stowe Devlin), Murvyn Vye (Waxie London), Vaughn Taylor (Ziggy Dawlt), Frank Ferguson (Mr. Shea), William Ogden Joyce (Bruce Cameron), James Todd (Mr. Hallerby), John Harding (Eduardo), Percy Helton (Charlie), Richard Collier (Homer), Edna Holland (Teacher), Betty Uitti (Sexy Girl), Lew Smith (Waiter), June Blair (Chorus Girl), Charles Wagenheim (Mike, the Bartender), Sid Kane, E. Molinari, and Bruno Della Santina (Waiters), Francesca Belloni (Flashy Woman), Paul Peterson (Joey), Gloria Pall (New Girl), Harry Hines, Gregg

J. Carrol Naish, Jean Simmons, Joan Blondell, and Neile Adams.

Martell, and Matty Fain (Mug Guests), Ray Walker (M.C.), Nora Marlowe (Mrs. Gretchma), Billy McLean (Man Contestant), Tim Graham (Official), Leonard Strong (Mr. Bernbaum), Len Lesser (Piano Tuner), the Archie Savage Trio, Ray Anthony and His Orchestra.

Anne Leeds, a schoolteacher from New England recently arrived in New York, takes a job after hours as a part-time secretary at the Tonic, a nightclub owned by a former bootlegger, Rocco, and his young partner and protégé, Tony Armotti. Anne's academic background and dignified manner delight the rough-hewn Rocco, but Tony feels that she is out of her element, as do some of the other people connected with the establishment. Little by little, Anne wins over her co-workers and the club's habitués, and although her new acquaintances try to protect her from the more unsavory aspects of the nightlife, Anne demonstrates she can take care not only of herself but also of the problems of others. Because of Anne's intervention, stripper Patsy St. Clair wins a cooking contest, busboy Hussein passes an algebra exam, and Rocco starts taking care of his diet. Only Tony, a philanderer who feels intimidated by Anne's propriety, doesn't openly display any affection for her. Determined to prove to him that a virtuous girl is not necessarily a dull one, Anne goes to Tony's apartment one night and confesses to being in love with him. When Rocco finds out about Anne's visit, he rebukes his partner for what he assumes is another of Tony's conquests. Anne leaves the Tonic for a position at another club, actually the front for a gambling joint, and is rescued by Tony when the police raid the place. The two make amends and Anne returns to the Tonic.

Percy Helton, Jean Simmons, Rafael Campos, and Paul Douglas.

Jean Simmons, Murvyn Vye and Anthony Franciosa.

RW:

    "They gave me the script to read. I thought it was a nice, little script but I could just see it being something that we would make a nice, little picture of and they would get it back East and the distribution people would say, 'That's great, but what are we going to do with it?' So I said I would pass on it. When the front-office people asked me if I didn't like the script, I told them, 'I think it's very funny and amusing. I

Producer Joe Pasternak, Anthony Franciosa, Jean Simmons, and Wise.

like the situations and I think Jean Simmons is excellent for it, but I don't want to spend six months working on something that will not get the right kind of promotion'. They said, 'No, no, no. We won't do that, it's going to be handled. They know we have it on the schedule and they love the idea.' So I said fine and went ahead with it. Passage of time. I'm in the midst of shooting *Until They Sail*, again with Jean. *This Could Be the Night* opened in New York and I was shown a review from the *New York Times* that said, 'A little MGM picture stole quietly into Loews State Theater yesterday and may turn out to be the sleeper of the season.' When I read that 'stole quietly,' I blew my top. I called my agent and said, 'Get me out of here, I want out of this place.' He called the studio and raised hell with them. I said, 'I don't work here anymore. I told you what was going to happen.' I still had time to go, but they did let me out with the proviso that I would give them another picture down the line, which turned out to be *The Haunting*.

"There were several scenes in *This Could Be the Night* set in the nightclub's kitchen, and I tried to make all the movement in and out of it very real. At that time, I used to be part-owner, with my brother Dave, of a restaurant up in Hollywood. I went there a few evenings and watched how the people went about their business in a kitchen. I did another thing I thought was good. We had so many scenes in the office while the musical numbers were going on outside that I wanted the actors to be aware that there was going to be music playing offstage. I didn't want, later in the dubbing process, to have to lower the music down terribly so that we could hear the dialogue. I did all my rehearsals with the playback going very loud so that the actors would have to get used to speaking up and playing in that fashion."

UNTIL THEY SAIL
(Metro-Goldwyn-Mayer, 1957)

Directed by Robert Wise. Produced by Charles Schnee. Associate Producer: James E. Newcom. Screenplay by Robert Anderson, based on a story by James Michener. Director of Photography (CinemaScope): Joseph Ruttenberg. Music: David Raksin. Title-song: music by David Raksin, lyrics by Sammy Cahn, sung by Eydie Gorme. Assistant Director: Ridgeway Callow. Special Effects: A. Arnold Gillespie, Lee LeBlanc. Art Direction: William A. Horning, Paul Groesse. Set Decoration: Edwin B. Willis, Henry Grace. Hair Styles: Sydney Guilaroff. Makeup: William Tuttle. Recording Supervisor: Dr. Wesley C. Miller. Film Editor: Harold F. Kress. 95 minutes.

Cast: Jean Simmons (Barbara Leslie Forbes), Joan Fontaine (Anne Leslie), Paul Newman (Captain Jack Harding), Piper Laurie (Delia Leslie), Charles Drake (Captain Richard G. Bates), Sandra Dee (Evelyn Leslie), Wally Cassell ("Shiner" Phil Friskett), Alan Napier (Prosecution), Ralph Votrian (Max Murphy), John Wilder (Tommy), Tige Andrews (Marine), Adam Kennedy (Lieutenant Andy), Mickey Shaughnessy (Marine), Patrick Macnee (Private Duff), Ben Wright (Defense), Kendrick Huxman (Justice), James Todd (Consul), David Thursby (Trainman), Hilda Plowright (Woman), Nicky Blair (1st Marine), Morgan Jones (2nd Marine), Jack Mann (Sergeant), Molly Glessing (Hotel Clerk), Pat Waltz (1st Marine), William Boyett (2nd Marine), Jimmy Hayes (3rd Marine), Alex Frazer (Mr. Hall), John Dennis (Sergeant), George Pelling (Steward), Owen McGiveney (Bank Official), Dean Jones (Marine Lieutenant), Robert Keys (Major Campbell), Ann Wakefield (Mrs. Campbell).

Jean Simmons and Joan Fontaine.

Like most New Zealand women, the four Leslie sisters of Christchurch have their lives radically altered with the departure of the country's able-bodied men to fight in World War II and the subsequent arrival of American servicemen in transit. Their father and brother are among the casualties, as is the husband Barbara only knew for a month. She later becomes involved with Captain Jack Harding, an American whose failed marriage left him scarred. The oldest sister, Anne is a spinster whose low opinion of the Americans changes when she falls in love with Captain Richard Bates. He dies before they can get married, never knowing that

Charles Drake,
Sandra Dee,
Joan Fontaine,
and Jean Simmons.

Piper Laurie,
Wally Cassell,
Sandra Dee, Joan
Fontaine, and
Jean Simmons.

Paul Newman and
Jean Simmons.

Anne is to bear him a child. The impulsive Delia marries a low-life, 'Shiner' Friskett, and, when he goes off to war, she moves to Wellington, engaging in several affairs with Yanks. Teenage Evelyn also flirts inconsequentially with Americans, but patiently waits for her boyfriend to return from the front. After her child is born, Anne moves to America and into the home of Bates' parents. With the end of the war, 'Shiner' returns home, and learning of Delia's infidelity, kills her. At the murder trial, Harding has no option but to testify against Delia's character, jeopardizing his relationship with Barbara, but in the end they remain together.

RW:

" I thought *Until They Sail* was a warm and human story, describing a rather unusual situation, and it touched me when I read it in Michener's book. I went to New Zealand in late 1956 with my art director, Paul Groesse, and the associate producer, Jim Newcom, who had been a top film editor and second-unit director. I needed to get a feel of the country and look for locations where Jim would shoot the background plates and long shots that were later worked into the film, which we shot entirely on the MGM backlot. In New Zealand, I met several women who lived through similar situations, getting firsthand information on the kind of love stories we were going to portray in the film. The ingredients of the drama were such that I knew I didn't have to bend on sentimentality. I hoped to make those stories, particularly the one with Paul Newman and Jean Simmons, as honest as I could without overdoing it. Jean is one of the best actresses I worked with. I don't think she ever was given enough credit for the quality of her acting. She was a star, but I think she should have been a much bigger one than she became. I thoroughly enjoyed doing those two films with her."

Cinematographer Joseph Ruttenberg, Joan Fontaine, Piper Laurie, Jean Simmons, and Wise.

RUN SILENT, RUN DEEP
(United Artists/Hecht, Hill and Lancaster, 1958)

Directed by Robert Wise. Produced by Harold Hecht. Associate Producer: William Schorr. Screenplay: John Gay, based on the novel by Captain Edward L. Beach. Director of Photography: Russell Harlan. Music: Franz Waxman. Technical Consultant: Rear Admiral Rob Roy McGregor. Special Photographic Effects: Howard Lydecker, Clifford Stine, Arnold Gillespie. Assistant Director: Emmett Emerson. Executive Production Manager: Gilbert Kurland. Art Direction: Edward Carrere. Set Decoration: Ross Dowd. Makeup: Frank Prehoda. Sound Recording: Fred Lau. Editorial Supervision: George Boemler. 93 minutes.

 Cast: Clark Gable (Commander Richardson), Burt Lancaster (Lieutenant Jim Bledsoe), Jack Warden (Mueller), Brad Dexter (Cartwright), Don Rickles (Ruby), Nick Cravat (Russo), Joe Moross (Kohler), Mary LaRoche (Laura), Eddie Foy III (Larto), Rudy Bond (Cullen), H. M. Wynant (Hendrix), John Bryant (Beckman), Ken Lynch (Frank), Joel Fluellen (Bragg), Jimmie Bates (Jessie), John Gibson (Captain Blunt).

In 1942, Commander P. J. Richardson had his submarine sunk by the Japanese destroyer *Akikaze* during a raid on Bungo Straits. After a year of desk work, he convinces the Navy Board to give him command of the U.S.S. *Nerka*, which antagonizes Lieutenant Jim Bledsoe, who had antici-pated the post. At sea, Richardson puts the crew through grueling drills designed to fire torpedoes while diving in the fastest possible time. Later, Richardson avoids confrontation with a Japanese submarine, leading to much speculation among the officers and crew. However, his drilling program proves efficient when the *Nerka* sinks an enemy destroyer with a bow shot in thirty-two seconds. Learning that, in defiance of orders, Richardson is heading for the Bungo Straits, Bledsoe confronts his superior. Richardson answers the accusation by saying it is his prerogative as Captain to alter the course. Once there, the *Nerka* meets a convoy protected by the *Akikaze*. The attempt to sink the de-

Burt Lancaster and Clark Gable.

stroyer is thwarted when a torpedo runs astray. The submarine is depth-charged, three crew members die and Richardson suffers a serious concussion. Bledsoe takes over and, after emergency repairs, the *Nerka* again

Burt Lancaster.

Burt Lancaster and Clark Gable.

Nick Cravat and Burt Lancaster.

faces the convoy. The *Akikaze* is destroyed. A cat-and-mouse game with another submarine ensues. With the ailing Richardson calling the shots, the Japanese submarine is blown to pieces. The effort was too intense for Richardson, and he dies. As the *Nerka* heads for home, Bledsoe and his men gather on deck to consign Richardson's body to the deep.

RW:

“ The biggest problem I had with *Run Silent, Run Deep* was that the screenplay was being rewritten all the way through. James Hill, a former screenwriter who had done some work for Harold Hecht and Burt Lancaster, was brought into their company, and it became Hecht, Hill and Lancaster. Harold Hecht was working on the screenplay with John Gay, but it was always being changed. I found out later, when I was shooting, that whereas Hecht and Gay would be working in the office, Hill and Lancaster were writing their own version. It was that kind of tug on the script all the way through. It got so bad that Clark Gable became concerned that maybe it was being slanted too much toward Lancaster, since it was Lancaster's company. We had a meeting one Saturday with Gable, his wife and his agent to reassure Clark that his part was not being taken away, that we were just trying to improve the script. He was fine after that.

"There was very good chemistry between Gable and Lancaster. Clark was an absolute dream to work with. He was always there at nine o'clock, ready to go for the first shot. After a one-hour lunch break,

he was all ready to go again. But at five o'clock he finished—that was in his contract. It had gone on for years that Gable never shot past five, but I did get him to do it for a few minutes once. I'd spent the whole afternoon rigging up a very difficult shot with water and tanks and things pouring. These shots are very time-consuming to set up. It was just getting ready to be shot a few minutes before five, and I knew if I didn't get it that day, I just had to start over in the morning and line it all up again. Clark had a couple of chums who had been with him for years, watching out for him, taking care of his clothes. I went to them, explained the situation, and asked them to convince Clark to stay a few minutes just to get this shot, and he did it. He said, 'Don't ask again,' but he stayed. One of the guys said to me, 'I'd never seen him do that before, no matter who.'

"All the underwater stuff was done with miniatures down at the Salton Sea. Part of that I was not around for because I had a little falling out with the company. When we finished shooting I did what I considered my cut and took a trip to New York for two weeks. When I came back, I found out that Burt Lancaster had sent for the film after I left and was playing around with the cut of it. By this time I'd had it. I said, 'It's his company, his picture, let him do what he wants.' I left and started work on *I Want to Live!* *Run Silent, Run Deep* is the only film I can remember where, when I was available, I didn't follow through all of post-production, but I don't think my cut was altered a great deal."

Susan Hayward.

I WANT TO LIVE!
(United Artists/Figaro, 1958)

Directed by Robert Wise. Produced by Walter Wanger. Screenplay by Nelson Gidding and Don Mankiewicz, based on articles by Ed Montgomery and letters of Barbara Graham. Director of Photography: Lionel Lindon. Music: Johnny Mandel. Jazz played by Gerry Mulligan, Shelly Manne, Art Farmer, Bud Shank, Red Mitchell, Frank Rosolino, and Pete Jolly. Assistant Director: George Vieira. Production Manager: Forrest E. Johnston. Art Direction: Edward Haworth. Set Decoration: Victor Gangelin. Costumes: Wes Jeffries, Angela Alexander. Makeup: Tom Tuttle, Jack Stone. Hair Styles: Emmy Eckhardt, Lillian Hokom Ugrin. Script Supervisor: Stanley Scheuer. Sound Mixer: Fred Lau. Film Editor: William Hornbeck. 120 minutes.

Cast: Susan Hayward (Barbara Graham), Simon Oakland (Ed Montgomery), Virginia Vincent (Peg), Theodore Bikel (Carl Palmberg), Wesley Lau (Henry Graham), Philip Coolidge (Emmett Perkins), Lou Krugman (Jack Santo), James Philbrook (Bruce King), Bartlett Robinson (District Attorney), Gage Clark (Richard G. Tribow), Joe de Santis (Al Matthews), John Marley (Father Devers), Raymond Bailey (Warden), Alice Backes (Nurse), Gertrude Flynn (Matron), Russell Thorson (San Quentin Sergeant), Dabbs Greer (San Quentin Captain), Stafford Repp (Detective Sergeant), Gavin MacLeod (Lieutenant), Peter Breck (Ben Miranda), Marion Marshall (Rita), Olive Blakeney (Corona Warden), Lorna Thayer (Corona Guard), Evelyn Scott (Personal Effects Clerk), Jack Weston (NCO), Leonard Bell (San Francisco Hood), George Putnam

Wise and Susan Hayward.

(Himself), Bill Stout (Newsman), Jason Johnson (Bixel), Rusty Lane (Judge), S. John Launer (San Quentin Officer), Dan Sheridan (Police Broadcaster), Wendell Holmes (Detective).

Academy Award winner for best actress. Academy Award nominations for best direction, adapted screenplay, cinematography in black and white, editing, and sound. New York Film Critics Circle Award for best actress. Golden Globe Award for best actress in a drama.

A woman of loose morals, Barbara Graham moves to Los Angeles after serving time on a perjury charge and starts working as a shill for two crooks, Emmett Perkins and Jack Santo. There is good money in the racket, but Graham gives it up to get married. Her husband, Henry, is a drug addict and their union collapses when she refuses to support his

Lou Krugman, Philip Coolidge, and Susan Hayward.

habit. With bills piling up and a baby to look after, Graham goes back to Perkins and Santo. Sometime later, the police arrest the trio, accusing them of the murder of an elderly woman, Mabel Monahan. Graham maintains her innocence, claiming she had spent the night of the crime with her husband and child. Unable to contact Henry and desperate to produce an alibi, she accepts an offer from a cellmate to buy the testimony of a certain Ben Miranda. During the trial, the fourth person charged with breaking into Mrs. Monahan's house, Bruce King, declares that Graham is solely responsible for the killing, and Miranda turns out to be a police officer. Graham is sentenced to the gas chamber. Ed Montgomery, an investigative reporter for the *San Francisco Examiner*, followed the case from the beginning, and, like other members of the press, capitalized on Graham's shady past and portrayed her as a vicious killer. While she awaits her execution, Montgomery, spurred by the opinion of psychologist Carl Palmberg that—despite being amoral—Graham is incapable of a violent crime, changes his point of view and starts a crusade to get her acquitted. His efforts, however, only succeeded in delaying the execution a number of months. The sentence is carried out June 3, 1955.

Virginia Vincent and Susan Hayward.

RW:

" I probably got more emotionally involved in that film than any other because of the nature of the story and the fact that I did talk to so many people about Barbara Graham. One of them was the priest who had been at the prison at the time she went to the gas chamber. He had left the prison not too long after Barbara's execution, and was the parish priest of nearby San Raphael. It was he who actually gave me the idea of how to treat the whole last act of the film cinematically. We all knew that it would consist of her arrival at San Quentin, her last night in the death cell, and the next morning with those stays and delays. What I didn't quite know was how to structure it. When I talked to the priest, I tried every way I could to see if I could get him somehow to say, perhaps inadvertently, what she had whispered in his ear when she stepped in the gas chamber, but he wouldn't let me know. During the course of our conversation, he said, 'I don't suppose that you have any idea of the terrible atmosphere that permeates a prison the day before, the night, and the morning of an execution. The whole prison knows that an execution is coming up, they know all the steps that are being made to take a human life.' The minute he said that, a light bulb lit above my head. I went right back to the prison and said, 'Show me everything that goes on from the moment you start to prepare for an execution until it's over— all the details, every routine you go through.' That gave me the spine around which to hook the last act.

"Then I saw an execution. I felt like a ghoul, asking to see it, but I felt that if I was going to deal with this matter of capital punishment, I wanted to be able to say to anybody commenting on the film that this is the way it is. I didn't want the reviewers to say, 'Well, that's a Hollywood version of what

Susan Hayward and John Marley.

goes on in the death cell and the gas chamber.' I didn't know whether I'd get sick or have to turn away. I was inside there with the warden. They brought in a young black fellow who had been convicted of killing a couple of white women, and, not unlike Barbara Graham, had run out of appeals and stays. I didn't know quite what to expect, but it was very calm, no hysterics. He went in and they did everything I described in the film. I found I was able to watch because it was so unemotional. It was awful, but I guess the worst thing is the fact that the body twists and turns and writhes for seven or eight minutes before it's finally pronounced dead. Of course, in the film we cut away very fast so as not to show a lot of it.

"I don't know to this day how I feel about Barbara Graham. After talking to some of the people who knew her, I'd feel she couldn't possibly have done it. Then I might talk to somebody a few days later and have another view of her. In spite of the kind of person she had become over the years, she had a quality about her that impressed people. Several people I met said there was something special about her, that if she had had a different background, she could have been a lady of real size and consequence. The thing we were trying to say was very well

Susan Hayward and Wise.

expressed in the papers the day after her execution. In almost every one of them, particularly on the West Coast, the sense of the editorials was that, no matter whether a person is innocent or guilty, nobody should ever have to go through the kind of torture that Barbara Graham went through, and that we should arrange our laws to protect anybody from that. That's what we wanted to say and not necessarily that an innocent person went to the gas chamber.

"I Want to Live! was made for Figaro, the company Joe Mankiewicz had formed under United Artists. Joe was not involved in the making of the film at all. In a way, he extended a helping hand to

Walter Wanger, who had an incident and spent time in jail himself and was trying to get started again.

"Shortly before we started to shoot, Joe came to a meeting with us. He liked the script generally, had a few points to make, some dialogue he felt could be better. He said, 'I think you're missing something here. You must make your point about capital punishment in the scene after the gas chamber, when her lawyer and the reporter meet outside and have that dialogue. You must raise this point.' We said, 'Joe, if our story hasn't been an indictment of capital punishment, then we failed miserably. We shouldn't have to talk about it now—the picture should have made the point.' He insisted, 'No, you've got to discuss it. You should lay your message in that exchange.' We fought it, but we had to give up—it was his company. Nelson Gidding wrote a couple of exchanges between the two, and I shot it in the exterior of San Quentin, but we never put it in the picture. We needed no statement at all.

"We had to compress and show as much of Barbara Graham's early life as we could—her background, how she developed, and what she became. And we needed to do it fast. She had this marriage, a baby was born, and they split up. I

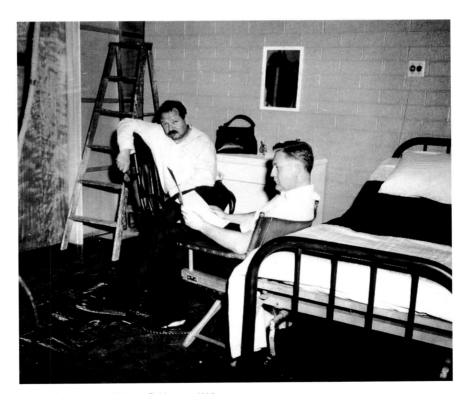

Screenwriter Nelson Gidding and Wise.

was looking for a way to cut out the obligatory middle scenes—they get married, they have a happy little honeymoon, then it starts to fall apart, and finally it breaks. I wanted to cut through that and show just marriage/baby/breakup. The scene ahead of that had Susan telling Phil Coolidge's character that she's going to be married. He's a little skeptical about it. She walks out and he's building a house of cards. I described the scene to my composer, Johnny Mandel, and said, 'He's building this house of cards and when she leaves, he shakes his head, pushes over the cards, and they fall. I move in the camera and I hold on those fallen cards, and I hold and I hold and I hold, way beyond the normal for a shot like that. Can you, Johnny, tell me over that long extra length of fallen cards about the dissolution of a marriage?' He said yes and I shot it that way, depending on the music. *I Want to Live!* was the only time I had a composer work on a film from the beginning because we needed the playbacks for the opening scene with Gerry Mulligan, Art Farmer, and other top jazz names, and also some pieces to be used when Barbara was playing the Victrola in prison.

"I usually cast my cinematographers for the look I want in the film. I saw *I Want to Live!* as having a very realistic, documentary feeling to it. I didn't want it to be too slick and polished. I had seen some of Curly Lindon's work at Paramount and decided he was right for it. Susan Hayward had another cinematographer in mind and that led to my only set-to with her. The photographer she wanted was very good, but used to making things look lovely and nice; he would not be on my list of candidates at all. We were in a stand-off on this. Finally, her agents told her to see me and try to get this very important matter resolved. I told her the cinematographer she wanted was wrong for the kind of picture I saw this being and held my line on it. She went back to her agents and they advised her to give in to me. She did, but she watched those dailies like a hawk all the way through. After the first couple of days, I thought I might lose Curly because she was complaining that her neck was not looking good, but we found ways of dealing with it that still fit the photographic approach we had for the picture."

ODDS AGAINST TOMORROW
(United Artists/Harbel, 1959)

Directed and Produced by Robert Wise. Associate Producer: Phil Stein. Screenplay by John O. Killens and Nelson Gidding (and, uncredited, Abraham Polonsky), based on the novel by William P. McGivern. Director of Photography: Joseph Brun. Music: John Lewis. Camera Operator: Sol Midwall. Assistant Director: Charles Maguire. Production Manager: Forrest E. Johnston. Script Supervisor: Marguerite James. Art Direction: Leo Kerz. Set Decoration: Fred Ballmeyer. Costumes: Anna Hill Johnstone. Makeup: Robert Jiras. Sound: Edward Johnstone, Richard Voriseck. Film Editor: Dede Allen. 95 minutes.

Cast: Harry Belafonte (Johnny Ingram), Robert Ryan (Ed Slater), Shelley Winters (Lorry), Ed Begley (Dave Burke), Gloria Grahame (Helen), Will Kuluva (Bacco), Kim Hamilton (Ruth), Mae Barnes (Annie), Carmen DeLavallade (Kitty), Richard Bright (Coco), Lou Gallo (Moriarity), Fred J. Scollay (Cannoy), Lois Thorne (Eadie), Wayne Rogers (Soldier), Zohra Lampert (Girl in Bar), William Zuckert (Bartender), Burt Harris (George), Ed Preble (Hotel Clerk), Mel Stewart (Elevator Operator), Marc May (Ambulance Attendant), Paul Hoffman (Garry), Cicely Tyson (Fra), Robert Jones (Guard), William Adams (Bank Guard), John Garden (Bus Station Clerk), Allen Nourse (Police Chief).

Harry Belafonte, Ed Begley, and Robert Ryan.

D ave Burke, an embittered ex-police officer who lost his job for re-
fusing to cooperate with a crime commission, plans to rob a small bank about 100 miles from New York City. In order to carry out his carefully detailed plan, he needs two accomplices. He contacts Ed Slater, a morose Southerner recently released from jail, and Johnny Ingram, a performer at a local gin mill with no criminal record. Ingram refuses to participate, even though he is heavily in debt because of his gambling habits. Burke persuades the man to whom Ingram owes money to collect, leaving Ingram with no choice but to go through with the deal. Burke and Slater drive to the small town of Melton, where the holdup will take place. Every Thursday the bank clerks stay after hours readying the payrolls for the various local factories. The robbers' access to the money is based on the fact that a black waiter from a drugstore brings coffee and sandwiches to the staff through a side door. Hearing that the third partner will be a black man, Slater, a deep-seated racist, has second thoughts. However, unable to find a job and tired of living off his understanding girlfriend, Lorry, he reconsiders. The first meeting of all three is charged with the animosity between Slater and Ingram, but Burke sets them straight. The trio converge at Melton on the assigned day. All goes well until Slater has to give Ingram the keys to the get-away car. He refuses, handing them to Burke instead. Burke is shot by a police officer while fleeing the bank, and Slater and Ingram, atop gas storage tanks, engage in a ferocious shootout that ends with a fiery explosion. Later, their charred bodies are placed side by side and the police cannot tell them apart.

Harry Belafonte and Ed Begley.

Robert Ryan and Shelley Winters.

Ed Begley, Robert Ryan, and Harry Belafonte.

RW:

66 The first person to do the screenplay was John Killens, a black
novelist who had never done a screenplay before. Harry
Belafonte was not fully satisfied with it and hired Abe Polonsky, one
of the writers who had been blacklisted in that awful McCarthy period
and had to write under pseudonyms. The script I read was done by
Abe. Of course I had no problems working with someone like him
because I so strongly opposed the blacklist and McCarthy's whole
viewpoint. I thought Abe was such a talent and marvelous to work
with. When we got closer to the shooting date, a polish needed to be done on the script and Abe was not available. Nelson Gidding was in New York working on a project with me and did it. When it came down to the question of credit, Abe's name still couldn't go on, unfortunately. We thought it wasn't right for Killens to have solo credit because his was not that much of a contribution. Nelson had worked considerably on it, so the final credit was decided by Harry and me to be that of Killens and Gidding, but a major part of the script I shot was Abe Polonsky's.

TOMORROW

AND

TOMORROW

AND

TOMORROW

YOU WILL REMEMBER THE EXCITEMENT
HE BRINGS TO THE SCREEN!

MEET ROBERT WISE, A MAN WHO WORKS WONDERS
WITH SUSPENSE. DIRECTOR WISE FIRST STARTLED THE
WORLD WITH AWARD-WINNING "I WANT TO LIVE"—AND
FROM THE ELECTRICITY IN THE AIR...THE WORLD HAS STILL
ANOTHER, AND EVEN GREATER JOLT COMING! IT'S CALLED
"ODDS AGAINST TOMORROW"
—AND BY ALL ODDS...YOU'LL NEVER FORGET IT!

COMING SOON!   THEATRE

UA

"I did something in *Odds Against Tomorrow* I'd been wanting to do in some pictures but hadn't had the chance. I wanted a certain kind of mood in some sequences, such as the opening when Robert Ryan is walking down West Side Street and on to Riverside Drive to go into the building, and particularly when they're in the town of Hudson [where we shot the fictitious town of Melton] as the night falls, the three men in different spots waiting for time to pass. I used infra-red film. You have to be very careful with that because it turns green things white, and you can't get too close on people's faces. It does distort them but gives that wonderful quality—black skies with white clouds—and it changes the feeling and look of the scenes. Years later, when I did *The Haunting*, I again used infra-red in some of the exterior shots of the house."

The Jets.

The Sharks.

WEST SIDE STORY
(United Artists/Mirisch/Beta, 1961)

Presented in association with Seven Arts. Directed by Robert Wise and Jerome Robbins. Produced by Robert Wise. Associate Producer: Saul Chaplin. Screenplay: Ernest Lehman. Book: Arthur Laurents. Music: Leonard Bernstein. Lyrics: Stephen Sondheim. Director of Photography (Technicolor, Panavision 70): Daniel L. Fapp. Musical Supervision: Saul Chaplin, Johnny Green, Sid Ramin, Irwin Kostal. Music Conducted by Johnny Green. Orchestrations: Sid Ramin, Irwin Kostal. Musical Assistant: Betty Walberg. Vocal Coach: Bobby Tucker. Choreography: Jerome Robbins. Dance Assistants: Tommy Abbott, Margaret Banks, Howard Jeffrey, Tony Mordente. Production

Designed by Boris Leven. Costumes Designed by Irene Sharaff. Assistant Director: Robert E. Releya. Photographic Effects: Linwood Dunn, Film Effects of Hollywood. Production Manager: Allen K. Wood. Production Artist: Maurice Zuberano. Titles: Saul Bass. Set Decoration: Victor Gangelin. Script Supervisor: Stanley K. Scheuer. Makeup: Emile La Vigne. Hairdresser: Alice Monte. Wardrobe: Bert Henrikson. Casting: Stalmaster-Lister Co. Music Editor: Richard Carruth. Sound: Murray Spivack, Fred Lau, Vinton Vernon. Film Editor: Thomas Stanford. Marni Nixon sings for Natalie Wood; Jimmy Bryant sings for Richard Beymer. Songs: "Jet Song," "Something's Coming," "Tonight," "Maria," "America," "One Hand, One Heart," "Gee, Officer Krupke!," "Cool," "I Feel Pretty," "Somewhere," "A Boy Like That," "I Have a Love." 155 minutes.

Cast: Natalie Wood (Maria), Richard Beymer (Tony), Russ Tamblyn (Riff), Rita Moreno (Anita), George Chakiris (Bernardo), Tucker Smith (Ice), Tony Mordente (Action), David Winters (A-Rab), Eliot Feld (Baby John), Bert Michaels (Snowboy), David Bean (Tiger), Robert Banas (Joyboy), Scooter Teague (Big Deal), Harvey Hohnecker (Mouthpiece), Tommy Abbott (Gee-Tar), Sue Oakes (Anybodys), Gina Trikonis (Graziella), Carole D'Andrea (Velma), Jose De Vega (Chino), Jay Norman (Pepe), Gus Trikonis (Indio), Eddie Verso (Juano), Jaime Rogers (Loco), Larry Roquemore (Rocco), Robert Thompson (Luis), Nick Covacevich (Toro), Rudy Del Campo (Del Campo), Andre Tayir (Chile), Yvonne Othon (Consuelo), Suzie Kaye (Rosalia), Joanne Miya (Francisca), Simon Oakland (Lieutenant Schrank), William Bramley (Officer Krupke), Ned Glass (Doc), John Astin (Glad Hand), Penny Santon (Madam Lucia).

Academy Award winner for best film, direction, supporting actor (George Chakiris), supporting actress (Rita Moreno), cinematography in color, art direction in color, editing, costume design in color, adapted score, and sound. Academy Award nomination for adapted screenplay. New York Film Critics Circle Award for best film. Golden Globe Award for best picture/musical, supporting actor (Chakiris) and supporting actress (Moreno) in a musical. Directors Guild of America Award for best direction. Writers Guild of America Award for best-written American musical.

The Jets and the Sharks are two rival gangs fighting for the same turf on New York's West Side. Riff, the leader of the Jets, challenges Bernardo, the leader of the Sharks, to a rumble during a dance at the gym, and asks Tony, with whom he founded the Jets, to join him. Tony, who wants no part in gang warfare, reluctantly agrees. The dance is also important to Maria, Bernardo's younger sister, recently arrived from Puerto Rico, who thinks of it as the real beginning of her life in America. Order reigns at the gym until Bernardo arrives with his girlfriend, Anita, and Maria and her finacé, Chino. The dance then turns into a fierce competition between the two groups. Tony arrives and from opposite sides of the hall exchanges glances with Maria. The two are immediately drawn to each other and come together in a dance that is interrupted by Bernardo.

Rita Moreno, George Chakiris, and Natalie Wood.

Maria is sent home and Tony, smitten by love, wanders the streets until he finds where she lives, and the two exchange love vows. The Jets and the Sharks hold a war council at Doc's candy store. Tony convinces the leaders to settle for a fist fight between the best man from each faction. The next day, Tony tells Maria that he has reduced the rumble to a one-on-one fight, but she makes him promise to stop it altogether. Bernardo and Ice are about to start the match when Tony intervenes, holding his hand out to Bernardo. Tony is thrown to the ground but still refuses to fight. Enraged, Riff attacks Bernardo. Knives are produced and Bernardo kills Riff. Disoriented, Tony grabs a knife and stabs Bernardo. The gangs quickly disperse. News of her brother's death reaches Maria shortly before Tony comes to her. Maria's love is stronger than her sorrow and she agrees to flee with Tony after he gets some money from Doc. When Maria is detained for questioning by Lieutenant Schrank, she asks Anita to tell Tony that she will meet him soon. Once at the candy store, Anita is taunted by the Jets. Livid, she delivers a different message: Maria has been killed by Chino. In desperation, Tony runs to the streets and challenges Chino, who was actually after him with a gun, to kill him, too. In the darkness, Tony sees Maria across the playground, but before he can reach her, Chino shoots him dead.

George Chakiris and Rita Moreno.

Richard Beymer and Russ Tamblyn.

WSS-13(5-33)

Co-directors at work—Jerome
Robbins and Wise in New York.

RW:

" We were in pre-production when I ran into Harold Mirisch one day and he asked, 'What would you think of having a co-director?' I said, 'What is that about?' He said, 'As you know, Jerome Robbins not only choreographed and directed the stage show, it's his concept. We had to go to him first about doing the choreography on the film, and he said that unless he can get involved in other aspects besides the choreography, he'd rather not do it.' I knew I could get his assistants to reproduce what he did on the stage, but Jerry is a special talent, so I said to Harold, 'Why don't you just let him direct it?' He said, 'No! This is a big, expensive film. We couldn't think of that.' I said, 'I don't see any way for a co-directing situation to work out.'

"I went home and started to think about it. I took off my director's hat and put on my producer's hat, and asked myself, 'What's the best thing for the film?' The answer was that if there's any possible way to get Robbins on the film, that would be the best thing. His assistants could reproduce what he had done on the stage, but in terms of adapting and creating new things for the screen, there was nobody like him. So I told Harold the next day that, in the interest of getting the best picture we could, I would certainly be open

Richard Beymer, David Bean, George Chakiris, and Russ Tamblyn.

to try and work out some kind of arrangement with Jerry. That started a series of meetings Jerry and I had trying to thrash out how we would do a compatible co-directing job on the film. It was soul-searching on both our parts. Finally, after a period of several months, we came to a meeting of minds. Jerry would be the prime director on all the musical aspects—the dancing and the songs. I would be there to help him whenever I could. I would be the director on all the book sections. He would, once again, be around to contribute what he could.

"Putting a stage musical on the screen represents challenges. When you're in the live theater, you have the proscenium arch up there, you're once-removed from reality. The screen is a very real medium and doesn't take kindly to stylization. One of the things we struggled with the most in *West Side Story* was how to take all the highly stylized aspects of it and deal with them effectively in the reality of the screen. On the stage, you can have characters break out of a dialogue scene and go right into song and dance and you don't feel a twinge of embarrassment, but you can feel that on the screen. On the stage, the turf that the kids fight over were stylized sets. There was no way I could realistically open the film without opening it in the real New York streets.

David Winters, Tony Mordente, Natalie Wood and Richard Beymer.

You can get away with sets at sunset or night, but when the sun is pouring down, you need the real thing. I felt that if I could do all the day shooting in New York, from then on we would be more successful in doing it back in Hollywood in sets at the studio or in Downtown Los Angeles. All the night street scenes were shot in Downtown L.A.; you can't tell the difference because you light just what you want to be seen. I had a hard sell with the Mirisch Company, but we were allowed to do it in the New York locations. Jerry said to me, 'I agree with you completely about the need to open it in New York, but you gave me the biggest challenge: to take my most stylized dancing and put it against the most real background that we have in the whole picture.'

"The aerial opening was also my concept. I knew I had to deliver New York, and I didn't want that same shot across the river, the bridge, and the skyline that had been shot to death. I had to find some new way. I started to think and to draw on myself from *Odds Against Tomorrow*. In it, I had to make a shot of Bob Ryan and Ed Begley in their car leaving New York City. I said to my assistant one morning, 'I wonder what those cloverleaves look like from the top of those apartment buildings on the other side of East River Drive.' He arranged for us to go up on the roof of one of the buildings, and we ended up using it. We shot kind of three-quarters down on East River Drive and the cloverleaves. I was thinking about that and I said to myself, 'I wonder what the canyons of New York look like straight down.' What I wanted to do was to show a New York that people hadn't seen, a different look of the city, almost an abstract one. I wanted to put the audience in a frame of mind to accept the kids dancing in the streets without feeling that twinge of embarrassment.

"When doing an adaptation, a lot of writers throw away as much of the original as they can to make the screenplay more their own. Ernie Lehman is not that way; he respects the original, incorporates all of its good values, and only tries to improve the weak areas. He has such a fine sense of construction. One of the first things he said to us on *West Side Story* was, 'The Officer Krupke number and the Cool number are in the wrong places.' In the original show, the Cool number was in the first act, before they have the council to set up the rumble. As they got a little nervous, they had the Cool number at the candy store to help settle down. The Krupke number, a comedy number, was done in the second act, after all the tragedy. This was all wrong. We simply switched them. Ernie did some rewriting to put the comedy number in the first act, before all the heavy drama started coming in, and then used Cool in a different and much better setting in the second act, to help pull the gang together when they're starting to fall apart. It's so much better dramatically. The only other major change we made was in the Somewhere number. On the stage show it was a dream, a fantasy ballet with a cloud backing and all. There's just no way to do that kind of thing on the screen. We didn't know, nor did Jerry, any way to retain that in the film. We struggled but couldn't come up with an answer, so we decided to do it in the simplest form possible.

"Jerry and I worked pretty well together for about sixty percent of the film, but we were getting behind schedule more and more and the company was getting very upset about this. We were pushing as much as we could, but they became convinced midway through that the co-directing situation was slowing things up. They finally insisted that Jerry go off the picture. It was a very uncomfortable, emotional, and difficult time for everybody, and certainly for Jerry. I was very unhappy about the development. I wanted it to work, but they thought we'd go better and faster if it was left up to just one person. Jerry had editing right in all the numbers he had done, so he stayed on and worked with the editor for a couple of weeks getting his cut of the numbers. When he finished, he came to me and said they were in the way they should be in, except for one. He didn't know what to do with it and asked me to take a look. Fortunately for us, Jerry had rehearsed all the other dance numbers himself. He had four assistants, and all but one stayed on the picture to help me get the dances on film. When I finished shooting, I got the picture in what I thought was a good first cut, called Jerry, and invited him to the studio. He saw the cut, liked the picture in general, had some criticisms and comments to make. I listened and accepted many of them. We got the picture out and he was up for the Academy Awards. It was an unfortunate development and a very touchy period for everybody, but the film turned out well and certainly Jerry's contribution to it is enormous, from every standpoint."

TWO FOR THE SEESAW
(United Artists/Mirisch/Argyle/Talbot, 1962)

Presented in association with Seven Arts. Directed by Robert Wise. Produced by Walter Mirisch. Screenplay: Isobel Lennart, based on the stage play by William Gibson. Director of Photography (Panavision): Ted McCord. Music: Andre Previn. Production Designed by Boris Leven. Costumes Designed by Orry-Kelly. Makeup: Frank Westmore. Sound: Lambert Day. Music Editor: Richard Carruth. Film Editor: Stuart Gilmore. "Song from Two for The Seesaw (Second Chance)" by Andre Previn and Dory Langdon. 120 minutes.

Cast: Robert Mitchum (Jerry Ryan), Shirley MacLaine (Gittel Mosca), Edmon Ryan (Taubman), Elizabeth Fraser (Sophie), Eddie Firestone (Oscar), Billy Gray (Mr. Jacoby).

Academy Award nominations for best cinematography in black and white and song.

Jerry Ryan, a lawyer from Omaha, has moved to New York after an emotionally crippling divorce. He interrupts his lonely roaming of the streets to go to a party at the apartment of a friend in Greenwich Village, where he overhears a conversation with a girl who introduces herself as

Shirley MacLaine and Robert Mitchum in the contiguous apartments.

Gittel Mosca. The next morning he calls her with the excuse of wanting to buy her refrigerator. They meet and begin to get to know each other. Gittel is a free-spirited aspiring dancer with a generous nature. She decides to let Jerry spend the night with her when she learns it's his birthday and that he is so in need of affection, but he slips out of her apartment. In the morning, he calls her, apologizes, and explains that he was afraid she was just being charitable. Jerry gets a well-paying job in Frank Taubman's law office and rents a loft for Gittel to practice her dancing and give lessons. One night, Gittel goes to a party alone. Jerry waits for her and sees her arrive home in a cab with an old boyfriend. He accuses her of unfaithfulness. Gittel, seemingly drunk, is actually suffering from a recurring ulcer pain. They have a violent argument. Jerry leaves, Gittel calls him back; her ulcer has hemorrhaged internally. Jerry rushes her to the hospital. When she returns home, Jerry nurses her and they become deeply involved. Gittel suggests that they marry after his divorce becomes final. He tells her that it has become final. Gittel, hurt and angry, asks Jerry if he can ever really commit himself to her. He decides to return home to his wife. Before leaving, he calls Gittel one last time.

Robert Mitchum and Shirley MacLaine.

Shirley MacLaine, Wise, and Robert Mitchum.

RW:

"It was interesting working with Robert Mitchum and Shirley MacLaine because they liked each other very much and set one another off in terms of telling stories, having fun, laughing. They were having such a good time trying to top each other that one of my biggest jobs as a director was to settle them down long enough to get them to do the scene. They were very funny; I was laughing as much as the crew. It got so bad that one day I called the crew back about twenty minutes early from lunch and had a little talk. I said, 'We have to stop being such a good audience for these two. They're so funny and amusing, I'm as guilty as you. But if we don't stop, we'll never get this picture done. We have to get a more serious tone on this set from now on and not go overboard in our laughter at their pranks.' They did settle down and we got the picture done, but I had to slow the crew down in terms of their reactions. The language was not the cleanest between the two. This was before today's very common use of four-letter words; they were not in everyday language then. The air used to get so blue around the set sometimes that I had to keep visitors off the stage; I was so embarrassed. But it was all good fun.

"One of the things that hooked me into doing *Two for the Seesaw* was the fact that Isobel Lennart wrote the screenplay. She was a wonderful lady, with a great sense of humor, and I had such a good experience working with her on *This Could Be the Night* that I thought it would be fun. She opened the play up where she felt it could be opened up. Sometimes you can be so concerned that you try to open too much and you lose what made it work originally. It seemed to me that what made the play work was seeing those two people up there in their own apartments and what was going on with their lives. It's a talky piece, it's all human contact and conflict, and it all took place in just the two apartments, which were side by side on the stage. That's a very difficult thing to do on the screen, and yet we felt

Wise scouts New York locations.

we should make a stab at it in a few places. That's why we came up with that set with the two apartments together, and I shot the film in Panavision so that I would have enough width to show it in certain shots. I was hoping to recapture that special feeling they had on the stage. Most people liked it, some carped about it. If it made it too theatrical, then I'm sorry—I thought it was the right approach."

A skecth by production designer Boris Leven for the opening of **Two for the Seesaw**, *and the scene as it appears in the film.*

THE HAUNTING
(Metro-Goldwyn-Mayer/Argyle, 1963)

Directed and Produced by Robert Wise. Associate Producer: Denis Johnson. Screenplay by Nelson Gidding, based on the novel "The Haunting of Hill House" by Shirley Jackson. Director of Photography (Panavision): Davis Boulton. Music Composed and Conducted by Humphrey Searle. Production Designer: Elliot Scott. Camera Operator: Alan McCabe. Special Effects: Tom Howard. Sketch Artist: Ivor Beddoes. Set Director: John Jarvis. Wardrobe Supervisor: Maude Churchill. Claire Bloom's Clothes: Mary Quant. Makeup: Tom Smith. Hairdresser: Joan Johnstone. Assistant Director: David Tomblin. Casting Director: Irene Howard. Continuity: Hazel Swift. Sound Recordist: Gerry Turner. Dubbing Mixer: J. B. Smith. Recording Supervisor: A. W. Watkins. Dubbing Editor: Allan Sones. Film Editor: Ernest Walter. 112 minutes.

Cast: Julie Harris (Eleanor Vance), Claire Bloom (Theo), Richard Johnson (Dr. John Markway), Russ Tamblyn (Luke Sannerson), Lois Maxwell (Grace Markway), Rosalie Crutchley (Mrs. Dudley), Fay Compton (Mrs. Sannerson), Valentine Dyall (Mr. Dudley), Diane Clare (Conie Fredericks), Ronald Adam (Eldridge Harper), Freda Knorr (Second Mrs. Crain), Janet Mansell (Abigail, age 6), Pamela Buckley (First Mrs. Crain), Howard Lang (Hugh Crain), Mavis Villiers (Landlady), Verina Greenlaw (Dora), Paul Maxwell (Bud), Susan Richards (Nurse), Amy Dalby (Abigail, age 80), Rosemary Dorken (Companion).

Claire Bloom, Russ Tamblyn, Julie Harris, and Richard Johnson.

A professor of anthropology with a fascination for the occult, Dr. John Markway is convinced that Hill House, a New England mansion with a history of deaths and strange occurrences, is the perfect setting for a scientific investigation of psychic phenomena. He leases the place and sets about choosing a group of people to help in the experiment. Of the many applicants, only two, Eleanor and Theo, both of them familiar with the supernatural, accept his invitation for a stay at the mansion. Eleanor had a childhood experience with poltergeists and Theo possesses startling extrasensory perception. The team is joined by Luke Sannerson, nephew of the owner of Hill House and a cynical skeptic. On their first night there, Eleanor and Theo are terrified by loud, pounding noises outside their bedroom door. Other eerie events convince Eleanor that Hill House is a living entity that wants her to stay there. A mousy woman who spent all her adult life caring for her invalid mother, Eleanor clings to this feeling of being wanted by the house as her last chance to break away

Claire Bloom and Julie Harris.

Wise and Julie Harris.

from her dingy existence. Her confused state of mind is compounded by her growing feelings toward Dr. Markway, and it is clear to the members of the group that she can no longer stay. As they try to talk Eleanor into leaving, Dr. Markway's wife, Grace, arrives unexpectedly. A pragmatic woman, she wants her husband to give up his experiments. When he refuses, she sets about proving her disbelief in the supernatural by spending the night in the nursery that is the psychic heart of the house. In the middle of the night, she is heard screaming but cannot be found. As the others look for Mrs. Markway, Eleanor is attracted to the library, where she climbs up a rickety metal staircase, from whose top a former maid at the house had killed herself. Dr. Markway saves Eleanor from harm and resolves to send her back. As she drives away, Eleanor loses control of the steering wheel and the car crashes against a tree. Eleanor dies at the same site as the first owner of Hill House.

Claire Bloom, Lois Maxwell, Richard Johnson, and Russ Tamblyn.

Richard Johnson, Julie Harris Claire Bloom, and Russ Tamblyn.

RW:

" I liked Shirley Jackson's book very much and was disappointed when United Artists, who had bought it for me, got a little cold on it and put it in turnaround. I was talking about it with my agent, and he reminded me that when I settled my contract with MGM in 1957, they made me promise that I would give them another picture down the line. I got the screenplay over to them while I was shooting *Two for the Seesaw*. They liked it and wanted to do it but would only spend a million dollars on it. We had their production department do a breakdown, and the best figure they could come up with was $1.4 million. Then somebody told me about the MGM studio in Borehamwood, outside of London; maybe they could do it for a better price in England. I met the fellows at the studio and they came back with a schedule that I could live with and a budget that came in at $1,050,000. That's how it turned out that the picture was entirely made in England. Still, I kept the New England background of the original story because I felt that the haunting of the house was fresher in the American scene.

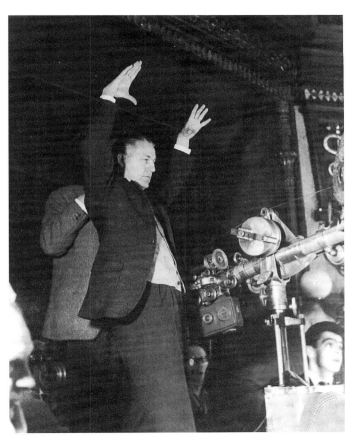

*Wise prepares an elaborate shot for **The Haunting**.*

"Regrettably, *The Haunting* was my last black-and-white film and I loved the look and style of it. All the interiors were designed by Elliot Scott and built on the Borehamwood lot. The exterior was a several-hundred-years-old manor house out in the country, about ten miles from Stratford-on-Avon. It was a pretty horrifying-looking thing under certain kinds of lights,

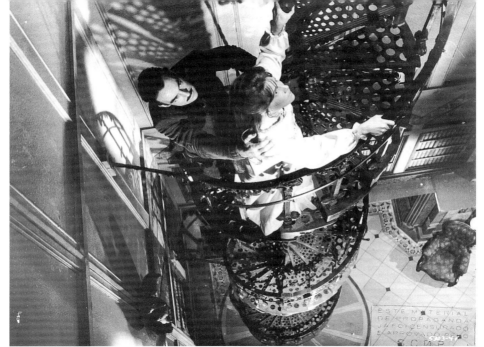

*Richard Johnson
and Julie Harris.*

5303-100

and I accentuated that by shooting some of the exteriors with infra-red film. I shot the film in Panavision and, at that time, there wasn't any wide-angle lens in anamorphic. The widest was maybe a 40mm. I wanted to make those hallways look long and dark and dank. I called the president of Panavision, Bob Gottschalk, and asked, 'Don't you have any wider-angle lens? I really want to get an almost unreal feeling about this house.' He said, 'We have developed a 30mm, but it's not ready for use yet. It's got a lot of distortion in it.' I said, 'That's exactly what I need for certain places—I want the house to look almost alive.' He didn't want to let me have it. I kept insisting and he finally relented on the proviso that I under-stood that it was not a finished lens and had distortions in it. I had to sign a document saying that I was willing to accept the extra amount of distortion and would never go back to Panavision and complain about it. I used it most effectively in just certain shots.

"The spiral staircase in the library was such an effective prop in the picture. It was scary when you were up on that thing and it was rocking around. The one shot we did on it that fascinates people the most is when the camera is at the bottom and goes up. We designed the banister of the stairway to be so wide and thick that it would fit a small rig with wheels on it—a little, light dolly that would hold a hand-held camera. We had our camera on that and we had a control wire underneath, all the way down. We simply took the camera up to the top on this rig, started it, rolled it down, and then reversed the film. It was all done on that balustrade. Another simple effect was the door that buckles. The door was all laminated wood, layers of wood on top of others. All I had was a strong prop man on the other side who would push it and move it. That's all it was and it scared the hell out of everybody.

"It's obvious in the story and what we put on the screen that Claire Bloom's character is a lesbian. We originally had a scene at the beginning with Claire in the bedroom of her apartment, and she's angry and yelling out the window at somebody. Then she goes and writes with lipstick on the mirror, 'I hate you.' I guess we caught a glimpse of the person in the car, showing it was a woman. Anyway, we established that this was a love affair with another woman. We thought that labeled it too heavily and hurt the scene, so we dropped it. It was better to let see it develop when Julie Harris turns to her in the scene out on the terrace and refers to her as being unnatural."

THE SOUND OF MUSIC
(20th Century-Fox/Argyle, 1965)

Directed and Produced by Robert Wise. Associate Producer: Saul Chaplin. Screenplay: Ernest Lehman. Book: Howard Lindsay and Russel Crouse. Music and Additional Lyrics: Richard Rodgers. Lyrics: Oscar Hammerstein II. Director of Photography (DeLuxe Color, Todd-AO): Ted McCord. Music Supervised, Arranged and Conducted by Irwin Kostal. Production Designed by Boris Leven. Choreography: Marc Breaux and Dee Dee Wood. Costumes Designed by Dorothy Jeakins. Puppeteers: Bil and Cora Baird. Assistant Director: Ridgeway Callow. Unit Production Manager: Saul Wurtzel. Special Effects: L. B. Abbott, Emil Kosa, Jr. Second-Unit Supervision: Maurice Zuberano. Makeup: Ben Nye. Set Decoration: Walter M. Scott, Ruby Levitt. Hair Styles: Margaret Donovan. Sound: Murray Spivack, Bernard Freericks. Film Editor: William Reynolds. Bill Lee sings for Christopher Plummer. Songs: "The Sound of Music," "Morning Hymn," "Maria," "I Have Confidence," "Sixteen Going on Seventeen," "My Favorite Things," "Climb Every Mountain," "The Lonely Goatherd," "Do-Re-Mi," "Something Good," "Edelweiss," "So Long, Farewell." 175 minutes.

Cast: Julie Andrews (Maria), Christopher Plummer (Captain von Trapp), Eleanor Parker (The Baroness), Richard Haydn (Max Detweiler), Peggy Wood (Mother Abbess), Charmian Carr (Liesl), Heather Menzies (Louisa), Nicholas Hammond (Friedrich), Duane Chase (Kurt), Angela Cartwright (Brigitta), Debbie Turner (Marta), Kym Karath (Gretl), Anna Lee (Sister Margaretta), Portia Nelson (Sister Berthe), Ben Wright (Herr Zeller), Daniel Truhite (Rolfe), Norma Varden (Frau Schmidt), Gil Stuart (Franz), Marni Nixon (Sister Sophia), Evadne Baker (Sister Bernice), Doris Lloyd (Baroness Ebberfeld).

Charmian Carr, Nicholas Hammond, Julie Andrews, Kym Karath, Duane Chase, Angela Cartwright, and Debbie Turner.

Academy Award winner for best film, direction, film editing, musical adaptation, and sound. Academy Award nominations for best actress, supporting actress (Peggy Wood), cinematography in color, art direction in color, costume design in color. Golden Globe Award for best picture/musical or comedy and actress in a musical or comedy. Directors Guild of America Award for best direction. Writers Guild of America Award for the best-written American musical.

A spirited young woman, Maria is a postulant at a nunnery in Salzburg, Austria. Her behavior is hardly in keeping with the austerity of her surroundings, and Mother Abbess gives her an opportunity to rethink her aptitude for a monastic existence by sending her to the home of a naval officer, Captain von Trapp, to be the governess of his seven motherless children. Once there, Maria quickly realizes that the Captain's military approach to raising his children has only succeeded in pulling them apart, and despite the siblings' attempts to scare her away, she soon gains their friendship. Disobeying the Captain's instructions, Maria adopts a more relaxed attitude with the children, taking them on field trips, teaching them to sing, bringing back the happiness they missed since their mother's death. Back home after an absence, the Captain brings with him an old friend, the musical promoter Max Detweiler, and the sophisticated Baroness, whom von Trapp plans to marry. A ball is organized to introduce the Baroness to the local society. As Maria and the Captain have a dance together, Maria realizes she is in love with him. Her feelings are no-

Christopher Plummer.

Eleanor Parker and Christopher Plummer.

ticed by the Baroness, and after a confrontation between the two, Maria returns to the convent. The children are disheartened, resisting the Baroness' feeble attempts to win them over. Maria explains to Mother Abbess her reason for quitting her job and is exhorted to pursue the dictates of her heart. She goes back to find that von Trapp requites her love. They marry. During their honeymoon, Max organizes the children into a

musical group, entering them in an annual competition, but von Trapp opposes having his family's singing ability exploited. On his return, the Captain receives an ultimatum to join the invading Nazi Navy. He refuses on patriotic grounds, and as the family tries to flee the country, they're intercepted by Nazi officers. Von Trapp pretends they are on their way to the musical festival and is told that as soon as the show is over, he is to be escorted to his new post. From the amphitheater they are able to make their way to the convent, and with the nuns' help head for the mountains and to safety in Switzerland.

Christopher Plummer and Julie Andrews.

RW:

" Right from the beginning, we felt that whatever we could do to diminish the overly saccharine aspects of it, and still not hurt the basic bottom line of the story and the emotional parts of it that touched and affected people, we would help ourselves. We made every effort to find ways of not getting too cute. We felt they overdid the folksy stuff in

the play, so we toned that way down. We purposely stayed away from all the cuteness of the castles that you could see all over the place in Salzburg and selected something very straight as the Captain's home. And we tried to do that as much as we could in the playing of it too. I'll never forget the first time Julie Andrews came over to have lunch in the dining room at Fox. Just as we sat down, she leaned over to me and said, 'How are we going to cut down all the sweetness that's in this piece?' I grabbed her hand and said, 'All I

Wise, Julie Andrews, and associate producer Saul Chaplin.

Wise and Julie Andrews.

can tell you is that we're talking the same language.' We still got accused by critics of being overly saccharine, but I think we really diminished a lot of it from the stage show.

"I can't remember us—Ernie Lehman, Solly Chaplin, and myself—talking about anybody else but Julie as the best possibility for Maria. There was some kind of underground buzz around town that maybe she wasn't quite as photogenic as she should be. She had not been seen on the screen yet, but she had just finished *Mary Poppins*, which was in the editing rooms. We made arrangements with the film's producer, Bill Walsh, to see a sequence or two with Julie. When she appeared on the screen, we knew we had to have her. For the Captain, I wanted Chris Plummer. I always felt that as portrayed on the stage, the Captain was a very obvious man, without any shading to him. I had seen Chris in a couple of plays in New York and I thought that he would give the Captain a little more substance, but I had a hard sell. He wasn't even interested in talking about it. At his agent's suggestion, I flew to London, had a meeting with him, and told him just how I thought it could be an interesting character with the kind of color he could give it. Only then he agreed to do it.

"There were two songs in the original show—'How Can Love Survive?' and 'No Way to Stop It'—done by the secondary couple, Max and the Baroness, that we felt didn't advance the plot at all. We wanted to drop those, as well as 'An Ordinary Couple,' the song Maria and the Captain sang when they fell in love. We felt we could get a more romantic piece there. Also, Ernie had an idea for what he thought would be a very good place for a new song, when Maria leaves the nunnery and tries to build her courage to face her job at the Captain's home. Of course, we had to talk to Richard Rodgers about it; Hammerstein was dead by this time. He had no problems with deleting the songs the other couple sang; they were not favorites of his. About 'An Ordinary Couple' he said, 'We wrote that toward the end, when we were finishing up. I think I can do something better than that for you.' When we told him about Ernie's idea for the new number, he thought it was excellent. Ernie had written some dummy lyrics just to get the sense over of what the number should say. Rodgers took the lyrics and rewrote them into 'I Have Confidence,' and wrote the new romantic number, 'Something Good.' Those were the major changes we made from the original

*Wise scouts locations for **The Sound of Music**.*

playbook. Ernie rewrote dialogue leading into songs in several instances so they could go smoothly in and not have that sense of embarrassment of suddenly going from dialogue into song.

"*The Sound of Music* was the first musical that had the songs dubbed into different languages. Musicals are not generally the most popular films in foreign countries. As a matter of fact, in the old days, they would cut a lot of the musical numbers for release overseas. We felt that by the very nature of the film and the storytelling propensities of the songs, they could really work this time. Solly Chaplin went abroad and spent several weeks going to Spain, France, Germany, and Italy, supervising the dubbing of the songs. Interestingly, of all the countries around the world, the film was least popular in Germany and Austria. I think that was because they were embarrassed by the Nazi element in the latter part of the film. Actually, during our location work in Austria, the filming of the scene with the troops marching through the plaza with the Nazi flags hanging out kept being pushed back on our schedule with increasing frequency. As we were getting close to the end of our stay there, I asked Solly Wurtzel, my production manager, 'What's all this delay about?' He said he couldn't get an okay from the City Hall to hang the flags out; they didn't want to be reminded of the Nazi period. I said, 'We all know what happened in Austria back then. We must have that.' Finally, he was able to persuade them to let us do it, but they were quite unhappy about it.

"The last location we did in Austria was Julie up on the hill doing the 'Sound of Music' number. Ernie had that opening described in the script. When I read it, I said to myself, 'Oh no! I can't do this same kind of helicopter shot as I did in *West Side Story*.' I called Ernie and said, 'We've got to get a different opening. Everybody is going to say we don't know anything to do except getting the helicopter to open our films.' Ernie said, 'I know what you mean, but I can't think of any other opening that I believe is right for this film. If you can think of one, be my guest.' After a week or two, I told Ernie, 'I give up. I can't think of anything that's nearly as effective. The hell with it. If it's right for the film, we'll just go ahead and do it.' The reaction to it was extraordinary.

Julie Andrews.

"I place as much importance on the production design as I do on the cinematography. This will sound like heresy to the cinematographers, but I think the production designer, if he's creative, can contribute as much to the look of the film as the cameraman. Boris Leven was a brilliant production designer and he did all my '60s films, with the exception of *The Haunting*. In the past, I had a situation where the production designer would bring the cinematographer a sketch of how a set was going to look. As an artist, he would naturally put a

Production designer Boris Leven's sketch for **The Sound of Music**.

light source in it to make it a good painting. The cinematographer would resent that, like the production designer was trying to tell him how to light a set. Several times I've seen a cinematographer look at the set sketch, put it away, and go his own way. My cinematographer on *The Sound of Music* was Ted McCord, with whom I had enjoyed working so much on *Two for the Seesaw*. Ted really loved Boris's ideas about lighting and they would often consult each other. Sometimes Ted would ask Boris to come out on the set and see what he thought about a certain approach toward lighting. After seeing the rushes at the end of the day, they'd walk back to their cars discussing what they had just seen. It was a very cooperative working relationship, which I value very much and had not always had between the production designer and the cinematographer.

"We thought we had a good chance at a successful film, but I don't think any of us anticipated that *The Sound of Music* was going to go through the roof like it did. It's a story about love, family, and togetherness. If there's one thing that people have in common in this world, it is the love for one another in terms of the family. That's the enduring quality of this story. Its tremendous success didn't become a burden to me. Obviously, one has to be very pleased and warmed by the spontaneous reactions that come up so often, in so many places around the world. That's most rewarding. The only slightly perverse thing about it is that it tends to make people forget and overlook some of the other films I've done that I'm very proud of, such as *The Body Snatcher, The Set-Up, The Day the Earth Stood Still, Executive Suite, The Haunting, Somebody Up There Likes Me, I Want to Live!,* and *The Sand Pebbles*. The film buffs know all those, of course, but the average viewers don't know the directors and their films. *The Sound of Music* tends to engulf some of the other equally good work I did. It doesn't overpower *West Side Story* so much, but I get many more comments about *The Sound of Music* than I do about *West Side Story*. The subject matter and the nature of *The Sound of Music* were more universally popular."

THE SAND PEBBLES
(20th Century-Fox/Argyle/Solar, 1966)

Directed and Produced by Robert Wise. Associate Producer and Second-Unit Director: Charles Maguire. Screenplay by Robert Anderson, based on the novel by Richard McKenna. Director of Photography (DeLuxe Color, Panavision): Joe MacDonald. Music Composed by Jerry Goldsmith. Music Conducted by Lionel Newman. Orchestrations: David Tamkin, Arthur Morton. Production Designed by Boris Leven. Production Associate: Maurice Zuberano. Unit Production Manager: Saul Wurtzel. Assistant Director: Ridgeway Callow. Second-Unit Photography: Richard Johnson. Special Effects: Jerry Endler. Set Decoration: Walter M. Scott, John Sturtevant, William Kiernan. Special Photographic Effects: L. B. Abbott, Emil Kosa, Jr. Costumes Designed by Renie. Wardrobe: Ed Wynigear. Technical Adviser: Harley Misiner. Makeup: Ben Nye, Bill Turner, Del Acevedo. Location Construction Supervisor: Herbert Cheek. Hair Styles: Margaret Donovan. Diversions by Irving Schwartz. Sound: Murray Spivack, Douglas O. Williams, Bernard Freericks. Film Editor: William Reynolds. 192 minutes.

Steve McQueen.

Cast: Steve McQueen (Jake Holman), Richard Attenborough (Frenchy), Richard Crenna (Captain Collins), Candice Bergen (Shirley), Marayat Andriane (Maily), Mako (Po-Han), Larry Gates (Jameson), Charles Robinson (Ensign Bordelles), Simon Oakland (Stawski), Ford Rainey (Harris), Joe Turkel (Bronson), Gavin McLeod (Crosley), Joseph di Reda (Shanahan), Richard Loo (Major Chin), Barney Phillips (Franks), Gus Trikonis (Restorff), Shepherd Sanders (Perna), James Jeter (Farren), Tom Middleton (Jennings), Paul Chinpae (Cho-Jen), Tommy Lee (Chien), Beulah Quo (Mama Chunk), James Hong (Victor Shu), Stephen Jahn (Haythorn), Jay Allan Hopkins (Wilsey), Steve Ferry (Lamb), Ted Fish (Wellbeck), Loren Janes (Coleman), Glenn Wilder (Waldron), Henry Wang (Lop-Eye), Ben Wright (Englishman), Walter Reed (Bidder), Gil Perkins (Customer).

Academy Award nominations for best film, actor, supporting actor (Mako), cinematography in color, art direction in color, original score, editing, and sound; Wise received the Irving G. Thalberg Memorial Award. Golden Globe Award for best supporting actor (Richard Attenborough).

Steve McQueen and Richard Attenborough.

Richard Crenna.

Steve McQueen and Candice Bergen.

hina, 1926. With the Communists and Nationalists fighting for power, the country is immersed in a civil war, and foreign nations with strong commercial and political interests in the outcome of the conflict mobilize their locally stationed armed forces. One of the instruments of the United States' gunboat policy is the U.S.S. *San Pablo*, a ship patrolling a section of the Yangtze River under the command of Captain Collins. A taciturn machinist who feels more at home with an engine than with other people, Jake Holman has just been transferred to the *San Pablo*. Immediately he incurs the antipathy of his crewmates when he expresses a dislike for having coolies do all the work onboard. Holman assumes full control of the engine room and strikes a cordial relationship with his assistant, Po-Han. The only other friend he makes on the ship is Frenchy. At a brothel, Frenchy falls in love with Maily, a beautiful girl who will be sold to the highest bidder. After unsuccessful attempts to buy her freedom, Frenchy takes Maily away. As the political situation worsens, Frenchy gets no shore-leaves. One night, he swims to the mainland to join Maily. When Holman looks for him the following day, he is told by Maily that Frenchy died of fever. The animosity toward the gunboat's crew reaches a peak when Holman's merciful killing of Po-Han—who was being tortured by the Nationalists—is manipulated for political purposes. Captain Collins is ordered to sail up river and help with the evacuation of American citizens. Among them is Shirley, a missionary whose tender relationship with Holman has blossomed into love. The *San Pablo* meets a heavily armed blockade, which is broken after a ferocious battle. At the mission, Collins' efforts to persuade the Americans to leave are in vain. As the landing party makes its way back to the *San Pablo*, fire erupts and Collins is killed. Holman takes over and loses his life while saving Shirley.

Steve McQueen and Candice Bergen.

RW:

"When I started planning the film, my first choice for Holman was Paul Newman. I had a list of five or six names and at the bottom was Steve McQueen, who I thought would be awfully good in it. I went after Paul, but he felt it was not for him somehow. When I mentioned Steve to the front-office people, they told me he was not big enough to carry such an expensive film. Then I got involved in *The Sound of Music*. By the time I got back on *The Sand Pebbles* in the latter part of 1964, Steve had had *The Great Escape* come out, which was a very popular film, and also *Love with the Proper Stranger*. I went back to the front office, and they told me that now it would be fine to have him as Holman.

"Of all the stars whom I worked with, I think Steve knew better what worked for him on the screen than any other. He had such a sense of what he could register, and that helped a lot in terms of shaping the character and the script.

"Steve could be a little moody—up some days, down a little on others. He always seemed to work a little bit on the

Wise and Steve McQueen.

end of his fingertips in the sense of his feelings about things, but he was fine. I only had one incident with him. I was on the boat one morning lining up a shot with the cameraman when Steve, who wasn't in this particular shot, came to talk about some wardrobe matter. I told him, 'I'm really involved in the shot right now. That wardrobe is not going to be used for several days, so let's talk about it later.' He went away and came back a couple of hours later, when I was really in a tense position on another shot. He said, 'Bob, that wardrobe . . .' I said, 'For Christ's sake, Steve! Can't you see I'm tied up in the shot? Let's talk about it at the end of the day.' Well, his feelings were so hurt that he didn't speak to me for three days. When I was directing the actor in a scene, he was fine, but he wouldn't say anything off the scene. We used to run our rushes every Sunday morning in the Army post theater in Taipei. That Sunday Steve came to see them and was thrilled. Everything was fine from then on and he started speaking to me again.

"*The Sand Pebbles* was the first time I worked on a film with major water scenes, and that drove me up the wall. Our gunboat was built from scratch in Hong Kong. It was designed with a flat bottom and under the rear deck there were two big diesel engines that actually propelled her for our picture purposes. In Taiwan, I shot in a river called Tam Sui. It was a tidewater river—about one mile out was the China Strait—so I had only a couple of miles of navigable water there, and when the tide was out, my boat would be sitting on the bottom. I had no way of getting the hundreds and hundreds of miles of the Yangtze River there, so all the additional shots of the *San Pablo* going up the various waters of the Yangtze were shot around the edges of Hong Kong and the mainland there. Hong Kong has no river, nor has the mainland at that point, but off the edge

Wise and camera crew set up a shot in Hong Kong.

of the mainland and the island are little spots of land. By very carefully placing the camera so that we had a bank on either side, we made it look like the river.

"It's very difficult working with boats in water. Every time we had to make another take, it took a long time to swing her around and get her back in the right position. We had a lot of weather problems in Taiwan. We would often go out with four, five different calls to shoot different scenes, depending on the conditions. If the tide was out, we had to try to shoot things on the deck where you wouldn't see the water. If it was a good day and the wind was blowing from the bow, I had to shoot a certain set of scenes because the smoke would have to match. If the wind was coming from the other way, I'd shoot another set of scenes. I'd have another call if the wind wasn't a factor. I'd have still another one if it was overcast; then I'd be doing a winter scene instead of a summer scene. If the weather was impossible and it rained, as it often did, we'd go inside a small studio in Taipei where we built some cover sets. We went on so long having trouble with the weather that we were running out of cover sets. We had already built the crew's quarters on the stage in Hollywood, but we got so scared of running out of work that the studio dismantled that set, flew it over to Taipei, and we eventually did all the scenes in the crew's quarters there.

"We were on the shooting schedule for eight and a half months, by far the longest I've ever been on. A great part of it was caused by the irrational weather. It was so frustrating some-times. When you go out on a day to shoot, it just kills you as a director not to get at least some kind of simple shot, even if it's just an insert. I went out there one day; it was a gray, moody day. There wasn't anything I could shoot. I wanted to get a shot of the stern of the boat with the American flag hanging against this dark, foreboding sky. That was the only thing I could think of shooting until the weather straightened out. We got the shot all lined up. The wind was blowing and we couldn't hold the *San Pablo*. We had a tugboat on one side trying to hold her. She was swinging back and forth, left and right, ruining everything. Just as we were about to turn the cameras on it, a puff of wind would come, or a cable would break, and she would swing. After two hours, I said, 'That's it! I've had it! Wrap everything up, get my shoreboat.' I just couldn't take it anymore. That was the only time I ever walked off a set. It was the most difficult location I ever tackled.

"I've often wondered if maybe I tried to tell too many stories in *The Sand Pebbles*. It was a multiple-story film—the story of the ship and the Captain, the story of Holman, the story of Frenchy and Maily, the story of the mission and the missionaries. I've wondered if, in terms of interest and length, I should almost have cut out the Frenchy/Maily story. Maybe I would have saved time, but I liked the story and thought that Dick Attenborough and Marayat Andriane were very touching. Also, I wanted to try to do the book and that was a very important part of it. You look back

*When **The Sound of Music** received Best Picture and Best Director Oscars, Wise was halfway across the globe shooting **The Sand Pebbles**. As the awards were announced, a celebration took place aboard the* San Pablo. *[bottom] Wise with his wife Pat.*

on films sometimes and if they have not been as all-out successful as you anticipated, you try to find reasons why maybe it didn't come off for audiences as well as you would have liked."

STAR!
(20th Century-Fox/Robert Wise, 1968)

Directed by Robert Wise. Produced by Saul Chaplin. Written by William Fairchild. Director of Photography (DeLuxe Color, Todd-AO): Ernest Laszlo. Music Supervised and Conducted by Lennie Hayton. Production Designed by Boris Leven. Dances and Musical Numbers Staged by Michael Kidd. Production Associate: Maurice Zuberano. Costumes Designed by Donald Brooks. Assistant Director: Ridgeway Callow. Dance Assistant: Shelah Hackett. Unit Production Manager: Saul Wurtzel. Special Photographic Effects: L.B. Abbott, Art Cruickshank, Emil Kosa, Jr. Set Decoration: Walter M. Scott, Howard Bristol. Hair Styles for Julie Andrews: Hal Saunders. Makeup: William Buell, William Turner. Wardrobe: Ed Wynigear, Adele Balkan. Sound: Murray Spivack, Douglas O. Williams, Bernard Freericks. Film Editor: William Reynolds. Original Songs: "*STAR!*," by Sammy Cahn and Jimmy Van Heusen; "In My Garden of Joy," by Saul Chaplin. Other Songs: "Down at the Old Bull and Bush," by H. Von Tilzer, H. Sterling, L. Hunting, and P. Krone; "Piccadilly," by Paul Morande, Walter Williams, and Bruce Seiver; "Oh, It's a Lovely War," by J. P. Long and Maurice Scott; "Forbidden Fruit," "Parisian Pierrot," "Someday I'll Find You," "Has Anybody Seen Our Ship?," by Noel Coward; "'N'Everything," by Buddy DeSylva, Gus Kahn, and Al Jolson; "Burlington Bertie from Bow," by William Hargreaves; "Limehouse Blues," by Philip Brahm and Douglas Furber; "Someone to Watch Over Me," "Dear Little Boy," "Do, Do, Do," by George and Ira Gershwin; "The Physician," by Cole Porter; "My Ship," "Jenny," by Kurt Weill and Ira Gershwin. 174 minutes.

Julie Andrews and Daniel Massey.

Cast: Julie Andrews (Gertrude Lawrence), Richard Crenna (Richard Aldrich), Michael Craig (Sir Anthony Spencer), Daniel Massey (Noel Coward), Robert Reed (Charles Fraser), Bruce Forsyth (Arthur Lawrence), Beryl Reid (Rose), John Collin (Jack Roper), Alan Oppenheimer (Andre Charlot), Richard Karlan (David Holtzman), Lynley Lawrence (Billie Carleton), Garrett Lewis (Jack Buchanan), Elizabeth St. Clair (Jeannie Banks), Jenny Agutter (Pamela), Anthony Eisley (Ben Mitchell), Jock Livingston (Alexander Woollcott), J. Pat O'Malley (Dan), Harvey Jason (Bert), Damian London (Jerry Paul), Richard Angarola (Cesare), Matilda Calnan (Dorothy), Lester Matthews (Lord Chamberlain), Bernard Fox (Assistant to Lord Chamberlain), Murray Matheson (Bankruptcy Judge), Robin Hughes (Hyde Park Speaker), Jeanette Landis (Eph), Dinah Ann Rogers (Molly), Barbara Sandland (Mavis), Ellen Plasschaert (Moo), Ann Hubbell (Beryl).

Academy Award nominations for best supporting actor (Daniel Massey), cinematography, art direction, costume design, adapted score, song ("*STAR!*"), and sound. Golden Globe Award for best supporting actor (Massey).

Richard Crenna and Julie Andrews.

Julie Andrews.

Julie Andrews and Daniel Massey.

In a screening room, Gertrude Lawrence watches a documentary on her life prepared by filmmaker Jerry Paul. It begins in Clapham, a London slum, in 1906, showing her first steps toward a music-hall career. At the age of seventeen, she seeks out her father, Arthur Lawrence, who had deserted her years before, and joins him in his act. Next she becomes a member of the Daffodil Girls, and then auditions for the famous Charlot Revue. She lands a part in the chorus and marries the company's stage manager, Jack Roper. Lawrence is pregnant when she gets her first big break—replacing the temporarily ill star of the show, Billie Carleton. When the star returns, Lawrence goes back to the chorus. Her marriage is short-lived, and she is soon seen frequently in the company of Sir Anthony Spencer, an admirer introduced to her by her lifelong friend Noel Coward. Under Sir Anthony's patronage, Gertrude Lawrence becomes a darling of the London society. Interested foremost in her career, she pushes aside his marriage proposal to become the star of Charlot's New York company. The show is a smash and, in no time, Lawrence is the toast of New York. Other successes follow while she fends off the romantic advances of a number of suitors. A French Riviera vacation with her daughter, who has lived away from her in boarding schools, ends in disappointment and Lawrence again plunges herself into work. Although she is one of the highest-paid stars in the theater, her extravagant lifestyle lands her in bankruptcy court. Working tirelessly to pay off her debts, she collapses and is taken to a hospital. Coward, as he had done several times before, lifts her sagging spirits with plans for a new show. At a surprise birthday party thrown by Coward, Lawrence insults one of the guests, Richard Aldrich. It is the stormy start of a relationship that will lead to a fulfilling union, one that comes to Lawrence at the time of her great triumph on the stage in "Lady in the Dark."

RW:

" It was never our goal to make the definitive biography. It was to be Gertie, her times, her successes, her problems, and, particularly, her musical life. We felt that the story of how she started and then became this highly popular theatrical personality was very interesting. We chose to end it at a certain point in 1940. In terms of definitive biography, we would have to go on to her death, but we didn't want to do that. We felt that the part of the story we needed to tell was the earlier part, up through and into World War II, when she met Richard Aldrich and seemed to be off and happily into a solid marriage. *STAR!* is more a recreation of the period and times of Gertrude Lawrence. It was not a literal copying at all because Julie Andrews could never do that. Gertie did not have a particularly good voice, but with her personality and acting ability she was very successful. We decided that Julie would just do a version of Gertie that would not conflict with her own musical qualities and talent. The conception from the beginning was that she would try to get as many as possible of the characteristics Gertie had: her determination, her feistiness, her kind of humor, her kind of anger.

"We had long-ranging years to show, so we knew we needed some kind of frame to tell the story and get through the gaps in time. After several sessions, we came up with the newsreel frame. I've been accused a few times of having stolen from *Citizen Kane*. That really wasn't a conscious thieving at all. As a matter of fact, I'd originally wanted to do some kind of animated frame. I'd seen something with animation, and it gave me a thought that maybe we could go from one section to another by doing a transition with animation. We tried to conceptualize this idea, but it didn't work and we got into doing the newsreel. That's a very tricky thing for the lab because the black-and-white images had to go into 70mm color for the final print. It had to be carefully treated to fit into the film without showing color.

"Because of the subject matter, it was decided that *STAR!* would open in London. We had a big première and the film went into the Dominium Theatre, the same theater that *The Sound of Music* had played for four years. The next day, the reviews came out. The first one I saw said, 'There goes the Dominium for another four years to Julie Andrews.' We felt we were off to a very commercial film, but it just didn't last. After coming back from London, the studio asked me to go to Australia to help with the kick-off there and do some publicity. Once again the film seemed to play very well with the audi-

Wise directing **STAR!**

ences at the premières, but I'm afraid it had the same kind of experience there as it had in London, New York, and Los Angeles. The audiences just didn't get caught up in it. When you have a hit like *West Side Story* or *The Sound of Music*, you have big word-of-mouth and a lot of repeat viewers, people who come back several times. *STAR!* didn't get the word-of-mouth and certainly didn't get the repeat viewers because after the first week it very steadily diminished and fell off at the box-office in a very surprising way.

"Some place down the line, the studio came to me a little hesitantly with a need, in their view, of trying to do something to salvage the film some way. They felt maybe the problem was the length. They thought that cutting some of the numbers, tightening it up, and making it considerably shorter, and perhaps even putting a new title on it, would change its fortunes at the box-office. As the filmmaker, I was reluctant to do this because we worked hard to make it. Yet, when you make a film that cost as much as *STAR!* did and it doesn't do business, you feel an obligation to let the company make an attempt to recoup the investment. So I gave my okay. They could have done it any-way, I didn't have final cut in it, but they did come to me. I didn't want to be involved personally in preparing the edited version. I found it too difficult to do. They cut it down to two hours and changed the title. It didn't do any better in the shorter version than it did before. *STAR!* is not the only film, by any means, that has had that kind of work done on it. That's hap-pened many times and rarely, if ever, made a successful picture out of one that wasn't doing the expected business.

"I've had films that haven't paid off, but *STAR!* was my biggest disappointment because I think it's a better film and more of an achievement than was acknowledged by the mass audience. People often ask me why it didn't work for them. It's hard to find the answers. Maybe they just weren't prepared to like Julie in the kind of character Gertie Lawrence was. Maybe we spent too much time on musical numbers and didn't spend enough time digging into her character, getting the kind of contact of the audience with what made her tick. With *The Sound of Music,* we certainly made contact with the audience in terms of the relationship between Maria and the children and the Captain. The audience knew where everybody was coming from basically. Another factor is that *Funny Girl* came out just a little ahead of us, and it's not a dissimilar film, and it was very successful. I often wonder what the reception would have been to *STAR!* if it had not been preceded by the opening and run-ning of *Funny Girl*, but that kind of thing we will never know."

THE ANDROMEDA STRAIN
(Universal, 1971)

Directed and Produced by Robert Wise. Screenplay by Nelson Gidding, based on the novel by Michael Crichton. Director of Photography (Technicolor, Panavision): Richard H. Kline. Music: Gil Melle. Production Designed by Boris Leven. Special Photographic Effects: Douglas Trumbull, James Shourt. Matte Supervisor: Albert Whitlock. Technical Advisers: Dr. Richard Green, George Hobby, William Koselka. Scientific Background Support by Cal Tech and The Jet Propulsion Laboratory. Scientific Equipment from Korad Lasers, Perkin-Elmer Corp., Central Research Labs Inc., R.C.A., Concord Electronics Corp., Du Pont Instrument Products Division, Van Waters & Rogers, Technicon Corp., Honeywell Corp. Costumes: Helen Colvig. TV by Hollywood Video. Production Manager: Ernest B. Wehmeyer. Assistant Director: Ridgeway Callow. Production Illustrator: Thomas Wright. Script Supervisor: Marie Kenney. Music Engineering: Allan Sohl, Gordon Clark. Art Direction: William Tuntke. Set Decoration: Ruby Levitt. Makeup: Bud Westmore. Hair Stylist: Carry Germain. Titles and Optical Effects: Universal Title, Attila De Lado. Animal sequences filmed under the supervision of The American Humane Association and Dr. W. M. Blackmore, D.V.M. Sound: Waldon O. Watson, James Alexander, Ronald Pierce. Film Editors: Stuart Gilmore, John W. Holmes. 130 minutes.

Arthur Hill, Wise, and James Olson.

Cast: Arthur Hill (Dr. Jeremy Stone), David Wayne (Dr. Charles Dutton), James Olson (Dr. Mark Hall), Kate Reid (Dr. Ruth Leavitt), Paula Kelly (Karen Anson), George Mitchell (Jackson), Ramon Bieri (Major Mancheck), Kermit Murdoch (Dr. Robertson), Richard O'Brien (Grimes), Peter Hobbs (General Sparks), Eric Christmas (Senator from Vermont), Susan Stone (Girl).

Academy Award nominations for best art direction and editing.

A space satellite falls to Earth in Piedmont, a desert village in New Mexico. The two military experts sent to retrieve it die mysteriously while searching the streets littered with bodies. This is the kind of emergency for which the Wildfire team was formed. It consists of a biologist,

Dr. Jeremy Stone; a microbiologist, Dr. Ruth Leavitt; a surgeon, Dr. Mark Hall; and a pathologist, Dr. Charles Dutton. Their mission is to identify and control the alien organism that caused the deaths. In Piedmont, Dr. Stone and Dr. Hall discover that the victims' blood has congealed to powder. They also find two survivors: a baby and a drunk old man. The group heads for a top-secret, five-story underground laboratory in the Nevada Desert that will self-destruct in case the virus spreads out. The youngest of the specialists, Dr. Hall is given the only key that can halt the laboratory's self-destruction. After thorough decontamination procedures, they reach the bottom floor of the installation and start the scientific investigation. The organism, christened the Andromeda Strain, is isolated. It is crystal-like in structure, lives on energy, and grows at a fast pace. Examining the survivors, Dr. Hall concludes that they escaped death because the old man's blood was too acid and the baby's too alkaline. Dr. Dutton gets trapped in a room contaminated with Andromeda. His survival proves that the virus has mutated to a benign form. However, as Andromeda breaks out of its container, the countdown to self-destruction starts. Dr. Hall makes a desperate run to avert it. His climbing of the core of the structure is made difficult by laser beams, but he reaches the mechanism in the nick of time.

James Olson, Arthur Hill, Kate Reid, and David Wayne.

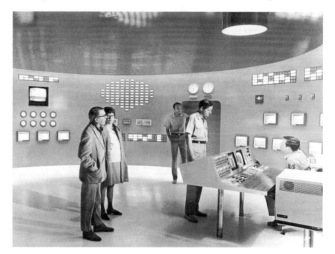

David Wayne, Kate Reid, James Olson, and Arthur Hill.

RW:

“ I never considered having Michael Crichton do the screenplay because I feel that, in most instances, the original author is so close to his book that it's hard for him to let go of something that needs to be dropped, and to condense and change things to make it work better in the script continuity. One of the qualities I like about Nelson Gidding—

Wise and cinematographer Richard H. Kline.

the same I like about Ernie Lehman—is that he has respect for the original work, and only tries to improve in areas that call for it. The one major change we made in *The Andromeda Strain* was Nelson's idea. One day, he came into my office and said, 'What would you think if we made the character Leavitt into a woman?' I blew up and said, 'Get the hell out of here with that kind of crazy idea. I can just see the reviews now: There's Raquel Welch in the submarine again.' He said, 'Wait a minute, hear me out,' and he described the kind of woman he saw as the scientist. He said, 'It's going to enrich the whole film. She's not Raquel Welch, she's an older woman with a biting, sarcastic sense of humor.' Nelson's idea paid off wonderfully. As played by Kate Reid, she turned out to be the most interesting character in the film.

"A very important sequence in the film is the one where they expose a monkey to the organism and it dies. The scene was vital in showing the deadliness of Andromeda, but I didn't know how I was going to do it—we couldn't kill a monkey. Jim Fargo, a second-assistant director on the film, said, 'I have some friends at the Veterinary Department at USC. I'll talk to them about the problem and see what they can come up with.' They thought about it and gave us the suggestion we used in the film. The set that the cage and the monkey were in was airtight. We filled the bottom of the set with carbon dioxide to the depth of three feet. When the cage door was opened, the monkey had no oxygen, only CO_2 to breathe. When he was almost gone, an assistant quickly grabbed him and passed him out to a veterinary doctor who was waiting just off the set. He flushed the monkey with oxygen from a stand cylinder and immediately revived him. All scenes with animals were shot with an SPCA supervisor on hand, and it was all done most properly.

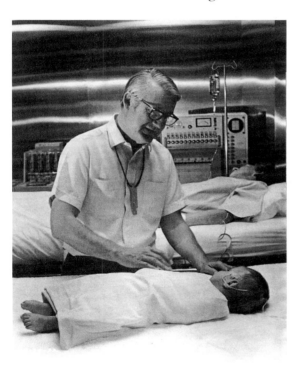

Wise and six-month-old Robert Soto.

"I thought *The Andromeda Strain* needed an underscoring, but it shouldn't be a standard background music score. I wanted it to be almost like sound effects. I listened to a number of people who were doing electronic music at the time and settled on Gil Melle. I told him that I didn't want anything in it that would sound like a musical instrument and yet I wanted it to serve like a background score would in a film. I needed to have an underpinning in a lot of instances with a kind of edge and nervousness to it to help heighten the tenseness of the film. I remember several times when Gil would deliver a cue and we'd look at it for the first time on the screen in the dubbing room. As we'd be going along, suddenly I would hear something that sounded like a violin note, or would hear a horn of some kind, something that was just musical to me. I would stop, call Gil, and say, 'That little passage in there sounds almost like music.' He'd go back and rework those bars and take out the musical sound. One of the pleasures of working with electronic music is that if you get a cue made and it isn't quite right, you don't have to worry about having to call the whole orchestra in again. The composer just goes over to his studio and redoes the cue.

Wise and Michael Crichton.

"*The Andromeda Strain* is more science fact than science fiction. In my research, I read an article about a biological-warfare base someplace in the desert in which there was a facility very much like ours that had been planned to be about seven stories underground, with one or two above ground. It ended up with only about three floors below ground. So they were planning and thinking, and did build a similar kind of thing. I liked the today-ness of the story, the fact that it dealt with technology and space, but the bottom line of what interested me in it was that I could make a film that was anti-biological warfare. I remember saying to Michael Crichton one day, 'One of the strong points, theme-wise, in this story is that it gives us a chance to make a statement against biological warfare. Not that I will lay on it heavily, but would you mind if I brought that up strongly in the screenplay?' He said, 'No. I always intended to do more with it in the book, but somehow I didn't get it. So if you make it more apparent in the screenplay, I'll like it very much.'"

TWO PEOPLE
(Universal/The Filmakers Group, 1973)

Directed and Produced by Robert Wise. Written by Richard DeRoy. Director of Photography (Technicolor): Henri Decae. New York sequences photographed by Gerald Hirschfeld. Music: David Shire. Production Designer: Harold Michelson. Production Manager from US: Ridgeway Callow. Production Manager from France: Enrico Isacco. Assistant Director: Denis Amar. Script Supervisor: Lucie Lichtig. Set Decoration: Eric Simon. Sound: Antoine Petitjean, Waldon O. Watson, Ronald Pierce. Lindsay Wagner's Wardrobe: Molly Harp. Makeup: Monique Archambault. Hair Stylist: Alex Archambault. Production Assistant in Morocco: Latif Lahlou. Assistant Director in Morocco: Larbi Bennani. Assistant and Interpreter in Morocco: Mohamed Abbazi. Film Editor: William Reynolds. 100 minutes.

Cast: Peter Fonda (Evan Bonner), Lindsay Wagner (Deirdre McCluskey), Estelle Parsons (Barbara Newman), Alan Fudge (Mr. Fitzgerald), Philippe March (Gilles), Frances Sternhagen (Mrs. McCluskey), Brian Lima (Marcus McCluskey), Geoffrey Horne (Ron).

*E*van Bonner, a young American living in Marrakech, meets with a representative from the American embassy, Mr. Fitzgerald, who makes arrangements for Evan to return to the United States. That same night, the two have dinner at a restaurant where fashion model Deirdre McCluskey is also present. On the train to Casablanca the next morning, Deirdre goes to Evan's compartment and is surprised to find him staring out of the window with tears in his eyes. They had not been introduced before, and once he gets a hold of himself, they strike up a conversation. When the train makes a stop for repairs, Deirdre and Evan realize that there is a growing attraction between them,

Estelle Parsons, Lindsay Wagner, and Peter Fonda.

but Evan rejects her advances. At the Casablanca airport, Evan is questioned because he has no passport, but a letter from Mr. Fitzgerald clears his way. While waiting for the plane that will take them to Paris, Evan

tells Deirdre that he is a Vietnam War deserter and that after three years in hiding, he has decided to give himself up and face court martial. They arrive in Paris, go their separate ways, but end up meeting again and spending the night together. The following morning, Deirdre tries to convince Evan not to return. He insists on going home and they fly to New York together. Evan spends the afternoon in the park with Deirdre and her son Marcus, leaving them later to turn himself in.

Lindsay Wagner, Brian Lima, and Peter Fonda.

RW:

" *Two People* was an original screenplay. When I read it, I thought it was a good love story but the by-product I was looking for was a way of indicting the Vietnam War from the American standpoint. I'm an anti-militarist and was very much against the Vietnam War, and I thought this story was another way of exposing what the conflict was doing to our young people, our young men in particular. There's a telling scene that takes place at night in Paris where Evan explains to Deirdre for the first time why he deserted, what his philosophical, intellectual, and emotional reasons were. I believed very much in it.

Peter Fonda, Alan Fudge, and Wise.

"I had done all the bigger films and I liked the modest size of *Two People*: small cast, small crew, entirely shot on real locations, not a foot of film done in the studio. With the exception of the scenes in New York, we shot it all with a French crew. I took with me just Harold Michelson as production designer and Reggie Callow as production manager. Our shooting followed the itinerary of the characters in the film. We started in Marrakech, then we literally shot on the train that runs from Marrakech to

Casablanca. From the railroad company we got one passenger car, which they allowed us to tear out a couple of compartments to make bigger shooting room, so we could shoot our scenes right on the car on the traveling train. We had no rear projection in the film at all. When we got to Casablanca, we were a little behind schedule. We had to get a charter plane to fly the whole company and the equipment back to Paris. We just barely got our shooting done, without the airport scene that was supposed to be in Casablanca. We ended up shooting it at the airport in Deauville, France. We filmed in Paris for four weeks. When we were finished there, we dropped our French crew and flew to New York, where we picked up a whole new crew and shot for a couple of days in an apartment and out in Central Park.

"I always knew that the kind of sparks and vibes between those two characters was terribly important to this particular story. They had to carry the whole thing—it's all about them. I was very conscious of that vital need, but you don't always know how that kind of thing is going to turn out. You have two people, you make tests of them, but you don't know whether that needed, built-in chemistry is going to be there. I thought Lindsay Wagner did an excellent job, and Peter Fonda was quite good. But I guess one of the reasons the picture didn't catch on as I hoped it would was that the chemistry just didn't come out right between the two. There's really nothing you can do about that as a director. It's an almost invisible thing; it has nothing to do with one's ability as an actor. Of course they were superb actors, but when you had Spencer Tracy and Katharine Hepburn together, the chemistry between them was marvelous. The same thing with Bill Powell and Myrna Loy; it's something that's inherent. Somehow, we didn't get enough sparks between Peter and Lindsay, and that's not a put-down of their respective jobs."

Wise on location in Marrakech.

THE HINDENBURG
(Universal/The Filmakers Group, 1975)

Directed and Produced by Robert Wise. Screenplay by Nelson Gidding. Screen Story: Richard Levinson and William Link, based on the book by Michael Mooney. Director of Photography (Technicolor, Panavision): Robert Surtees. Music: David Shire. Song: "There's a Lot to Be Said for the Fuehrer," music by David Shire, lyrics by Edward Kleban. Special Photography: Clifford Stine. Special Visual Effects: Albert Whitlock. Special Mechanical Effects: Glenn Robinson, Frank Brendel, Andrew Evans, Robert Beck. Production Designed by Edward Carfagno. Technical Adviser: George Lewis. Matte Photography: William Taylor. Costumes Designed by Dorothy Jeakins. Continuity Illustrator: Tom Wright. Unit Production Manager: Ernest Webmeyer. Set Decorations: Frank McKelvey. Stunt Coordinator: John Daheim. First Assistant Director: Howard Kazanjian. Second Assistant Director: Wayne Farlow. Makeup: Del Acevedo, Frank McCoy, Rick Sharp. Hair Styles: Lorraine Roberson. Sound: Leonard Peterson, Don Sharpless. Film Editor: Donn Cambern. 125 minutes.

George C. Scott, Rene Auberjonois, Roy Thinnes, Burgess Meredith, and Anne Bancroft.

Cast: George C. Scott (Colonel Ritter), Anne Bancroft (The Countess), William Atherton (Boerth), Roy Thinnes (Martin Vogel), Gig Young (Edward Douglas), Burgess Meredith (Emilio Pajetta), Charles Durning (Captain Pruss), Richard A. Dysart (Lehmann), Robert Clary (Joe Spah), Rene Auberjonois (Major Napier), Peter Donat (Reed Channing), Alan Oppenheimer (Albert Breslau), Katherine Helmond (Mrs. Mildred Breslau), Joanna Moore (Mrs. Channing), Stephen Elliott (Captain Fellows), Joyce Davis (Eleanore Ritter), Jean Rasey (Valerie Breslau), Ted Gehring (Knorr), Lisa Pera (Freda Halle), Joe di Reda (Schulz), Peter Canon (Ludecke), Charles Macaulay (Kirsch), Rex Holman (Dimmler), Jan Merlin (Speck), Betsy Jones Moreland (Stewardess Imhoff), Colby Chester (Eliot Howell III), Teno Pollick (Frankel), Curt Lowens (Elevator Man Felber), Kip Niven (Lt. Truscott), Michael Richardson (Rigger Neuhaus), Herbert Nelson (Dr. Eckener), Scott Walker (Gestapo Major), Greg Mullavey (Morrison), Val Bisoglio (Lt. Lombardi), Simon Scott (Luftwaffe General), William Sylvester (Luftwaffe Colonel), David Mauro (Goebbels), Joseph Turkel (Detective Moore), Sandy Ward (Detective Grunberger).

Special Achievement Academy Awards for visual effects and sound effects. Academy Award nominations for best cinematography, art direction, and sound.

May, 1937. Concerned with repeated threats against the dirigible *Hindenburg*, the German government assigns Luftwaffe Colonel Franz Ritter to conduct investigations aboard the vessel as she sails to Lakehurst, New Jersey, in her first transatlantic crossing of the season. In his scrutiny of passengers and crew, Ritter is assisted by Martin Vogel, a Gestapo agent. As the airship leisurely flies to its destination, the two probe potential saboteurs: the Countess, an old friend of Ritter's, at odds with the Nazi regime; Edward Douglas, a businessman who is frequently sending and receiving coded telegrams; Albert Breslau, caught by Ritter trying to smuggle diamonds; Joe Spah, a music-hall artist who openly scorns Hitler; and Emilio Pajetta and Major Napier, two professional card sharks. Ritter's strongest suspicions, however, fall on a crew member: First Rigger Boerth, whose mistress, Freda Halle, is put under surveillance in Germany. Evidence corroborates Ritter's hunch, and he confronts Boerth, telling him that Freda has been arrested. Boerth admits to being a member of a resistance movement against the Third Reich and says he has hidden a time-bomb that will destroy the dirigible after everyone has safely disembarked. Rain at Lakehurst delays the landing and Ritter asks Boerth to set the bomb for 7:30 PM, thus

Burgess Meredith and Anne Bancroft.

giving passengers and crew enough time to leave the ship. Bad weather further delays the landing, and Vogel uses brute force to extract information from Boerth. Frantically scouring the ship for the bomb, Ritter finds the barely conscious Boerth and is told where the device is located. At 7:22 PM, Ritter finds the bomb. As he attempts its deactivation, it goes off. The flames quickly reduce the *Hindenburg* to a mass of aluminum, killing thirty-five of the ninety-seven people on board.

RW:

"Universal approached me about taking over a project
they were developing about the *Hindenburg*. As I read
about it, I got all caught up in the whole concept of the
lighter-than-air ship and became fascinated with the fact that
you could be flying in great ease and comfort in this lovely
flying machine. I decided to pursue it. However, I knew we
were going to depend heavily on the fine use of a big minia-
ture model, as well as traveling mattes and all kinds of background and trick shooting. So before I took on the project, I
went to talk to Al Whitlock, the master matte artist. I asked
him, 'Are we going to be able to convincingly show the
Hindenburg on the ground outside of a hangar in Frankfurt,
take her off, get her up in the air, fly her over land and over
the ocean, bring her in past New York City, bring her down
to Lakehurst, and get her ready to land when she blows up?' I
told the studio that I would like to have a crack at it only
when I had his assurance that it could be done.

"Filmmaking is a learning experience. With *The
Hindenburg*, I became one of the world's great authorities on
lighter-than-air ships.
My research started at
the Smithsonian
Institution in Washing-
ton. Eventually, I went
to Berlin and contin-
ued it there. One of
the problems with the
Hindenburg was that
all its plans had been
lost in the war. Eddie
Carfagno was my
production designer,
and he had the
challenge of building
the sets only from
descriptions and some
sketches that were in
books. We needed to
get every bit of
material that we possibly could to help us recreate her. We
went to museums in Berlin and Munich. From Munich we
drove to Friedrichshafen, where she was actually built. They
had quite a lot of memorabilia there. We got dozens of
photographs, measurements, and figures to help Eddie in

Wise and production designer Edward Carfagno.

designing all the interior sets, as well as helping Al and the modelmakers to make the big twenty-seven-foot model.

"One of the major decisions we had to make on the picture was about using the actual newsreel material for the big disaster. We talked about it, analyzed it, and felt that those were such extraordinary pieces of film that if we tried to reproduce them, as skilled as our technicians are, we couldn't really come close to capturing what they were able to capture in the real thing. Plus we found that these films had been so widely seen over the years that it would be difficult for us to overcome the impression they had already made on the viewers. It just seemed to us that we should find a way to use the actual footage. The only reason it happened to be extensively covered was that this was the maiden voyage of the *Hindenburg*'s second year. If it had been the second or the third trip, there wouldn't be any cameras out there. In other days, we probably would have shot the film in black and white because we

Wise and George C. Scott.

were going to use black and white newsreels for the tragedy at the end, but by this time color was the thing and Universal wouldn't hear of a film, certainly one of this size and cost, being shot in black and white. So we just decided to go in color for the body of the film and find a way to get into black and white for the end.

"Then came the question of how to fully dramatize what might have gone on inside the ship from the time the explosion started until she was on the ground. We got the idea of taking a section of the actual newsreel, going to a certain point, and stop-framing it; then we would cut to our scenes of what was happening to the people in the different parts of the ship. After a few minutes, we would go back to another section of the newsreel, stop it again and return to the people inside. That's how we stretched out the minute and a half of the actual disaster to make a full-blown sequence of the tragedy. However, when you have a concept like this, you are never completely sure how it's going to work. Just to protect ourselves, I shot all the film to cut into the actual crash in color, in case our concept

Anne Bancroft and Wise.

didn't work and we had to recreate the crash. Then we had to degrade the color to black and white, and further degrade the black and white so it could match the grainy newsreel footage. We had something like 700 opticals in that whole sequence.

"I always bristled a little when people said, 'Well, you're getting on the cycle of disaster films.' It really wasn't that. I'd say, 'Usually the disaster happens in the first reel or two, and you spend the rest of the story with how people deal with it. We have a whole ten reels of picture before it happens; our disaster comes at the very end. We're building to it.' Our challenge was how to hold the interest and keep the audience in enough involvement until we got to the disaster. I guess with some people it did work, and with some it didn't. I got all fascinated by the whole idea of the lighter-than-air ship, how it worked, what the experience was. Maybe that was such an overpowering thing in my mind that I didn't come up with enough

Cinematographer Robert Surtees and Wise.

of the human and emotional components that audiences respond to. But I'm proud of *The Hindenburg*. It's quite an achievement to make it believable the way we did."

AUDREY ROSE
(United Artists, 1977)

Directed by Robert Wise. A Robert Wise Production. Produced by Joe Wizan and Frank De Felitta. Screenplay: Frank De Felitta, based on his own novel. Director of Photography (Metrocolor, Panavision): Victor J. Kemper. Music composed and conducted by Michael Small. Production Designer: Harry Horner. Production Manager: Charles Maguire. Orchestrations: Jack Hayes. Consultation on Hypnosis: Jean Holroyd, Ph.D. Court Technical Advisor: Daniel A. Lipsig. Costumes Designed by Dorothy Jeakins.

Anthony Hopkins, Susan Swift, and John Beck.

Special Effects: Henry Millar, Jr. Production Illustrator: Maurice Zuberano. Set Decoration: Jerry Wunderlich. First Assistant Director: Art Levinson. Second Assistant Director: Leslie Moulton. Camera Operator: Bob Thomas. Script Supervisor: Marie Kenney. Makeup: Fred Griffin. Hairdresser: Jean Austin. Sound: Tom Overton, William McCaughey, Aaron Rochin, Michael J. Kohut. Music Editor: Milton Lustig. Film Editor: Carl Kress. 113 minutes.

Cast: Marsha Mason (Janice Templeton), Anthony Hopkins (Elliott Hoover), John Beck (Bill Templeton), Susan Swift (Ivy Templeton), Norman Lloyd (Dr. Steven Lipscomb), John Hillerman (Scott Velie), Robert Walden (Brice Mack), Philip Sterling (Judge Langley), Ivy Jones (Mary Lou Sides), Stephen Pearlman (Russ Rothman), Aly Wassil (Maharishi Gupta Pradesh), Mary Jackson (Mother Veronica), Richard Lawson (Policeman #1), Tony Brande (Detective Fallon), Elizabeth Farley (Carole Rothman), Ruth Manning (Customer in Store), Stanley Brock (Cashier in Store), David Wilson (Policeman #2), David Fresco (Dominick), Pat Corley (Dr. Webster), Eunice Christopher (Mrs. Carbone), Karen Anders (Waitress).

Janice and Bill Templeton lead a happy life in New York City until a stranger starts prowling the school attended by their twelve-year-old daughter, Ivy, and following Janice and the child to their apartment building. One day, the stranger introduces himself as Elliott Hoover and explains the reason for his behavior. In 1965 he had lost his wife and little daughter, Audrey Rose, in a car accident, the girl having been burned alive. After the tragedy, Hoover sought solace in meditation and during a stay in India, learned of the realities of reincarnation. Since then, he became obsessed with finding the person who would be holding the soul of his beloved daughter. Convinced that Ivy—born just minutes after Audrey Rose's death—is this person, Hoover pleads with Janice to help him free the tortured soul from the girl. The Templetons dismiss Hoover's story as the ravings of a lunatic, but Ivy's recurring nightmares of being burned make Janice believe that maybe there is truth in what he said. One night, Hoover, hoping to alleviate Ivy's suffering during one of her nightmares, forcibly takes her to his apartment. Bill sues Hoover for kidnapping. In the course of the trial, Janice, now certain of

Marsha Mason, Susan Swift, and John Beck.

Hoover's good intentions, disagrees with Bill's conduct and the couple become estranged. Irate, Bill authorizes a regression-through-hypnosis experiment guided by Dr. Lipscomb that will be accepted as evidence in court. Ivy is taken back in time until she relives Audrey Rose's terrifying demise. Unable to return to the present, Ivy dies during the session.

RW:

" I interviewed many candidates for the role of Ivy and wound up testing four of them before deciding on Susan Swift, who was not experienced in film at all. It was such a demanding part that I felt I could use some help. I heard about a young actress/teacher/coach named Joan Darling, who was supposed to be very good in working with novice actors. I talked to Joan about my problem, and I felt she could work ahead of time with Susan, making her understand what she had to bring out in the scenes where she's rather taken over. Joan coached her before we started and worked with her occasionally before scenes. I don't mean to imply by this that something was wrong with Susan, but it was such a challenging role for a little ten-year-old girl that I felt perhaps a woman with experience as an actress might be an asset to me in getting the very best out of Susan.

"Because of our schedule and the fact that so much of the story happened between the four people, we were able to put

*Wise on the set of **Audrey Rose**.*

a week's rehearsal ahead of the actual shooting. I made a requirement that the set be finished and dressed, so I could go in with the actors and a few crew members and rehearse all the important scenes, blocking them out. It's always a big help when you have a chance to do that. Not just read through the script, but actually rehearse the scenes to see how they play. The reason you don't get to do that in movies is because it costs money. The minute you call actors in for a rehearsal, you have to start paying them. According to the picture's schedule, a key actor may not appear until the fourth or fifth week of shooting. That means that if you rehearse with him, you're going to have to pay him for a whole month. That's very hard for studios to accept. In this particular instance, it just meant paying those four for an additional week. *Audrey Rose* is the only film in which I had a full week of rehearsal before shooting.

"We had a sequence in the bedroom between Marsha Mason and John Beck in which they get to a very high, angry pitch, and it wasn't right somehow as written in the script. I suggested that at the end of the day's shooting we get John and Marsha into the bedroom and just let them improvise the scene to see what they could come up with. They got into a really tough argument, much better than the one we had. Frank De Felitta had a tape recorder and he taped everything. Later, he went back to his office and rewrote the entire scene, taking elements that the actors had come up with in the improvisation. That's one of the few times I've ever done that kind of thing and it worked."

STAR TREK—THE MOTION PICTURE
(Paramount, 1979)

Directed by Robert Wise. Produced by Gene Roddenberry. Associate Producer: Jon Povill. Screenplay: Harold Livingston. Story: Alan Dean Foster. Director of Photography (Metrocolor, Panavision): Richard H. Kline. Music: Jerry Goldsmith. Special NASA Science Adviser: Jesco Von Puttkamer. Special Science Consultant: Isaac Asimov. Special Photographic Effects Directed by Douglas Trumbull. Special Photographic Effects Supervisor: John Dykstra. Special Photographic Effects Produced by Richard Yuricich. Production Designer: Harold Michelson. Executives in Charge of Production: Lindsley Parsons, Jr., Jeff Katzenberg. Unit Production Manager: Phil Rawlins. Assistant Directors: Danny McCauley, Doug Wise. Costume Designer: Robert Fletcher. Art Directors: Joe Jennings, Leon Harris, John Vallone. Set Decorator: Linda DeScenna. Senior Illustrator: Michael Minor. Illustrators: Maurice Zuberano, Rick Sternbach. Makeup Artists: Fred Phillips, Janna Phillips, Ve Neill, Charles Schram. Hair Stylist: Barbara Kaye Minster. Special Effects (Non-Optical): Alex Weldon. Supervising Sound Editor: Richard L. Anderson. Special Musical Assistance: Lionel Newman. Music Editor: Ken Hall. Special Animation Effects: Robert Swarthe. Mechanical Special Effects: Darrell Pritchett, Ray Mattey, Marty Breslin. Titles: Richard Foy/Communication Arts Inc. Graphics: Lee Cole. Sound Editors: Stephen Hunter Flick, Cecelia Hall, Alan Murray, Colin Waddy, George Watters III. Property Master: Richard Rubin. Sound Effects Created by Dirk Dalton, Joel Goldsmith, Alan S. Howarth, Francisco Lupica, Frank Serafine. Sound Mixer: Tom Overton. Film Editor: Todd Ramsay. 132 minutes.

Wise, Gene Roddenberry, William Shatner, DeForest Kelley, and Leonard Nimoy.

Cast: William Shatner (Admiral James T. Kirk), Leonard Nimoy (Mr. Spock), DeForest Kelley (Dr. Leonard "Bones" McCoy), James Doohan (Montgomery "Scotty" Scott), George Takei (Sulu), Majel Barrett (Dr. Christine Chapel), Walter Koening (Chekov), Nichelle Nichols (Uhura), Persis Khambatta (Ilia), Stephen Collins (Commander Willard Decker), Grace Lee Whitney (Transporter Chief Janice Rand), Mark Lenard (Klingon Captain), Marcy Lafferty (Chief DiFalco), Billy Van Zandt (Alien Ensign), Ralph Brannen, Ralph Byers, Iva Lane, Franklyn Seales, and Momo Yashima (Bridge Crew), David Gautreaux (Commander Branch), Michele Ameen Billy (Epsilon Lieutenant), Roger Aaron Brown (Epsilon Technician), John D. Gowans (Transporter Assistant), Jon Kamal (Lieutenant Commander Sonak), Leslie C. Howard (Yeoman), Michael

Rougas (Lieutenant Cleary), Junero Jennings (Engine Room Technician), Sayra Hummel (Engine Room Technician), Howard Itzkowitz (Cargo Deck Ensign), Rod Perry (Security Officer), John Dresden (Security Officer), Edna Glover, Paul Weber, and Norman Stuart (Vulcan Masters), Paula Crist (Crew Member), Terrance O'Connor (Chief Ross), Gary Faga (Airlock Technician), Joshua Gallegos (Security Officer), Doug Hale (Computer Voice/Off Camera), Susan J. Sullivan (Woman in Transporter).

Academy Award nominations for best art direction, original score, and visual effects.

*I*n the twenty-third century, members of the Starfleet who monitor station Epsilon 9 witness, startled, the annihilation of three patrolling Klingon spaceships by an awesome field of force. Information is sent to the Starfleet headquarters in San Francisco that the unknown aggressor has entered Federation territory and is heading toward Earth at incredible speed. The newly refurbished Starship U.S.S. *Enterprise* is ordered back into immediate service to meet the emergency. Its former Captain,

Persis Khambatta, Stephen Collins, Leonard Nimoy, and William Shatner.

James T. Kirk, now promoted to Admiral and relegated to a bureaucratic position, persuades his superiors to return the command of the ship to him. This causes immediate friction between Kirk and his successor, Captain Willard Decker, who has to resign himself to being Kirk's assistant. Reunited in the 431-person crew are Kirk's old companions of past missions, Mr. Spock and Dr. Leonard "Bones" McCoy. Among the new members is Navigator Ilia, a friend of Decker's from planet Delta. With time ticking by, the *Enterprise* flies at warp speed until it comes within the orbit of the enemy. The ship is taken over by the entity, and Ilia is abducted. She is later returned to the *Enterprise* and informs Kirk that, unless the entity—V'Ger—meets its creator, it will destroy the Earth. When Kirk, Spock, McCoy, and Decker follow Ilia to V'Ger's core, they discover that it actually is a space probe, Voyager 6, launched in the twentieth century to collect information. With all the data it accumulated, V'Ger developed into an intelligent being that now wants to unite with its creator to attain human qualities. Fascinated by the prospects of such a melding, Decker joins Ilia and offers himself to V'Ger. With Earth's safety assured, the *Enterprise* flies to new adventures.

RW:

“ Paramount had planned *Star Trek* as a major movie for television. Then they decided to make a feature film. They had a script written but it needed a lot of work. Michael Eisner, who was heading the studio, told me they wanted to start shooting in April of 1978. I said, 'If that's an absolute requirement, I won't accept the assignment. There's a tremendous amount of preparation to do. Nothing has been done about all the special effects that are needed.' Eisner's reasoning was that they had the actors under contract. When the start date for the TV film came, they had to ask for a delay and give the actors some money. Then they had to do that again. Now if they didn't start in April, they were going to pay them some more. I said it was impossible to begin it in April, and we worked that out. Finally, at some point around June, when we had to get another delay, therefore costing more money for the actors, the studio said, 'That's the last one—you have to start shooting early in August, ready or not.' So we started in August with only the first act of the script in the kind of shape that is on the screen. The rest of it was still not worked out. We knew generally where we were going, but the script was being rewritten all the way up to the very last day of shooting. Harold Livingston had been brought on to do the new versions of it; Gene Roddenberry always had his own versions; and the actors, particularly Leonard Nimoy and William Shatner, had their own concepts about what the scenes should be like as related to their established characters. It was a three-ring circus in some ways. At the last few days of shooting, the scenes were being rewritten so much that I was getting three sets of changes a day.

Wise and Douglas Trumbull.

"Early on, we tried to get all the very complicated special effects sorted out. Robert Abel & Associates had been signed to do them before I came on it. Bob was very successful in doing all kinds of special effects for TV commercials, but he had never done anything of the size of *Star Trek.* They had brilliant people and great concepts, but they were very slow-going in a practical sense. The long and the short of it is that when I started to shoot the film, I had nothing in the way of special effects that I could show to my actors. All the scenes where they're sitting in the control cabin and looking at the big screen, I had nothing up there. What they were looking at was a target, to see that their eyes were all in the same direction, and I was off-camera reading out of the script what was going to be happening up there. Of course, in science-fiction films you have a lot of special-effects material that only goes in after you finish shooting, but we didn't have anything at all.

"Then we had a lot of very special shooting to do on the set with the Bob Abel company, and they took an awful long time. They were on all through the shooting, without really making the kind of progress that I felt should be done. Very close to the end, all of us were getting more and more concerned about their ability to get all this work done in the time we needed. Paramount had already committed the film to be in a thousand theaters in December of '79 as their big Christmas feature. Finally, I insisted that they show us what they had. We had a running and I was very unhappy with the results. I went back to the studio and said that I didn't think they were going to be able to meet our deadline, and they were taken off the film.

"The studio had persuaded Doug Trumbull, who had done the special effects for *The Andromeda Strain* for me, to come on and be a consultant, guiding Abel and his people. Some other picture he was planning on doing fell through, and we were able to get Doug and his company to do the special effects we needed. Because it was too big a job for just one outfit, we also got John Dykstra and his Apogee Company. Trumbull and Dykstra decided who would do what, splitting up the work. We finally did get it all put together in good shape, but since these men came on late, it meant that they had

Leonard Nimoy and Wise.

to work their plants and their people almost around the clock, seven days a week. We had a tremendous amount of work to do, and those visual effects take such a long time. As a result of this, the cost just exploded in terms of that whole end of the budget. All the way along, every aspect of the production just grew in enormous size. *Star Trek* did very big business, but it cost a tremendous amount. All the stretching out, all the delays, all the problems with the shooting on the set and with the special effects, having to go to new people midstream and having them work around the clock, pushed its cost to around $40 million.

"Science-fiction films are very challenging to do because of all the non-human elements that you have to deal with, and yet they're all related to humans. *Star Trek* was a very trying experience because I had so many things that were beyond my control in terms of special effects. And then there were times when hours and hours would go by with very tricky lighting, which was when we got to the actual Voyager. That was a tremendous set, and some of the setups took hours just to light. Also, it's always rough if you have to start on a picture—and particularly a big, complex one like *Star Trek*—with a script that's not completed. The only other time I had any kind of serious ongoing rewrite was on *Run Silent, Run Deep*, but not as much as *Star Trek*. It's not a good experience. That is, for the kind of film I make and the kind of filmmaker I am. Of course, there are people who do make up and write, to a degree, as they go along. That's not my style and I don't find it satisfactory at all."

ROOFTOPS

(New Visions, 1989)

Directed by Robert Wise. Produced by Howard W. Koch, Jr. Co-Produced by Tony Mark and Sue Jett. Co-Producer: Allan Goldstein. Executive Producers: Taylor Hackford and Stuart Benjamin. Screenplay: Terence Brennan, based on a story by Allan Goldstein and Tony Mark. Director of Photography (DeLuxe Color): Theo Van de Sande. Music Score by David A. Stewart and Michael Kamen. Production Design: Jeannine C. Oppewall. Choreography: John Carrafa. Capoeira Choreography: Jelon Vieira. Unit Production Manager: Edwin (Itsi) Atkins. First Assistant Director: Alex Hapsas. Second Assistant Director: Joseph Ray. Costume Design: Kathleen DeToro.

Troy Beyer and Jason Gedrick.

Script Supervisor: Cornelia Rogan. Location Manager: Brett Botula. First Camera Operator: John Sosenko. Art Director: John Wright Stevens. Production Illustrator: Brick Mason. Set Decorator: Gretchen Rau. Special Effects Coordinators: Candy Flanagin and Steve Kirshoff. Wardrobe Supervisor: Barbara J. Hause. Key Makeup Artist: Anne Pattison. Hair Stylist: Aaron F. Quarles. Film Editor: William Reynolds. Songs: "Avenue D," by David A. Stewart and Etta James; "Drop," by George Chandler, Jimmy Chambers, Jimmy Helms and Liam Hensall; "Freedom," by Pat Seymour; "Rooftops," by David A. Stewart, Pat Seymour, and Richard Feldman; "Keep Running," by Robert Reed and James Avery; "Loving Number One," by Vince Hudson and June Hudson; "Revenge (Part I)," by David A. Stewart and Annie Lennox; "Stretch," by Charlie Wilson and David A. Stewart; "Meltdown," by David A. Stewart and Michael Kamen; "Bullet Proof Heart," by Grace Jones and Chris Stanley. 95 minutes.

Cast: Jason Gedrick (T), Troy Beyer (Elana), Eddie Velez (Lobo), Tisha Campbell (Amber), Alexis Cruz (Squeak), Allen Payne (Kadim), Steve Love (Jackie-Sky), Rafael Baez (Raphael), Jaime Tirelli (Rivera), Luis Guzman (Martinez), Millie Tirelli (Squeak's Mom), Robert La Sardo (Blade), Jay M. Boryea (Willie), Rockets Redglare (Carlos), Edouard de Soto (Angelo), John Canada Terrell (Junkie Cop), Bruce Smolanoff (Bones), Edythe Jason (Lois), Paul Herman (Jimmy), Lauren Tom (Audry), Stuart Rudin (Wino), Robert Weil (Hotel Clerk), Coley Wallace (Lester), Jose Inoa (Young Cook), Danny O'Shea (Rookie Narc), Herb Kerr III (Jorge), Kurt Lott (Zit), Peter Lopez (Burn), Jed James (X), Woodrow Asai (Yard Foreman), Angelo Florio (Cop at Dance), Diane Lozada (Older Sister), Imani Parks (Young Sister).

High above New York's Alphabet City streets, a group of homeless kids create their own living spaces on the rooftops of abandoned tenement buildings. Among them is T, a loner, orphaned at an early age, whose home is a water tower. T supports himself by stripping remnants from derelict buildings and selling them for scrap. In his spare time, he

hangs around the Garden of Eden, a vacant lot in the neighborhood where his friends gather to listen to music and practice Combat Dance, a friendly contest in which the winner drives his opponent out of a platform without touching him. One night at the Garden of Eden, T meets beautiful Elana, who is visiting with a friend. The attraction is mutual but their relationship is jeopardized by the fact that Elana works as a

Troy Beyer and Jason Gedrick.

lookout for her cousin Lobo, a drug dealer who takes over the building on top of which T lives and converts it into a crackhouse. When police officers bust the place, Lobo blames T and has one of his henchmen burn the water tower. The following day, T is badly hurt in a fight with Lobo. While T recuperates, his young friend Squeak, known in the area for his graffiti murals, defies Lobo's power and is killed by the drug dealer. Enraged, T uses his newly acquired knowledge of the Brazilian martial art capoeira to confront Lobo. With the help of Elana and his friends Amber, Kadim, and Jackie-Sky, T attracts Lobo to the rooftop, where Lobo steps on rickety ground and falls to his death. That night, the Garden of Eden is the setting for a joyful celebration.

RW:

“ What particularly attracted me to the original script for *Rooftops* was that it dealt with the timely issue of homelessness from the perspective of the youths who live on the streets. Somehow, whenever this subject is approached, the kids with no families who have to fend for themselves are rarely mentioned. I also liked the energy of it and the fact that I would be working with young people. The combat dance was always an integral part of the script, but the capoeira was an afterthought. Taylor Hackford became very taken with this ritualistic martial art from Brazil. In story conferences, he

Troy Beyer and Wise.

Wise and Kurt Lott.

Alexis Cruz and Wise.

insisted that we should try and incorporate capoeira sequences into our story. Howard Koch, Tony Mark and I were very much against it. We kept fighting, Taylor kept insisting and Terence Brennan kept rewriting until we finally got the version that's in the film. I think Terence did as good a job as possible at accommodating capoeira, but we ended up with a script that was too manu-factured. The film became a hybrid: it has too much dancing that isn't intrinsic to the story, and it isn't realistic enough. Yet, I was very unhappy with the critical comparisons that were made between *Roof-tops* and *West Side Story.* *Rooftops* is not a musical, it is a romantic drama with music and dance. The leading characters don't sing and the dancing is not used to advance the story."

PROJECTS

• 1946: Wise and Val Lewton planned a color version of Joseph Sheridan Le Fanu's classic vampire novella *Carmilla,* which was to be transposed to colonial America.

• In mid-1958, Nelson Gidding started writing the screenplay for a film based on the life of celebrated war photographer Robert Capa. He worked on it in New York while Wise was making *Odds Against Tomorrow,* for which Gidding contributed revisions and script polishing. The finished screenplay, titled *Battle! The Lives and Wars of Robert Capa,* was picked up by the Mirisch Company, but budget considerations and demands made by Capa's family ultimately killed the project, which Wise tried to get off the ground for several years. He explains: "It's one of those things I loved very much but just couldn't bring on. We were going to tell the story of Capa's covering the wars primarily through the use of his photographs in what we called photodramas. Nelson and I dreamed up a new approach in telling World War II and all with just photographs, voice-over, sound effects, and music."

• 1965: Wise's company, Argyle, bought film and TV rights to Laura Lee Hope's popular series of children's books *The Bobbsey Twins.* A feature, to be written by Allen Vincent, with story consultation by Frances Marion and songs by Sammy Fain and Paul Francis Webster, was to be followed by a TV series.

• 1966: Argyle acquired rights to Anais Nin's 1954 novel *A Spy in the House of Love,* which was to be scripted by Barbara Turner and produced by Jerry Bick.

• 1968: Robert Wise Productions developed a TV special about Mae West, which failed to attract network interest.

• 1971: Wise's first project for The Filmakers Group, then based at the Columbia studios, was an adaptation of Eliot Asinof's book *Craig and Joan,* a non-fiction account of the suicide pact between two New Jersey teenagers. The screenplay was written by Nelson Gidding.

- 1971: *Time and Again*, Jack Finney's time-travel book, intrigued Wise because of its fanciful premise and the opportunity it would give him to recreate the New York of the late 1800s. The high budget required to bring it to the screen deterred potential backers.

- 1973: Michael Wilson prepared a treatment for *Stranger at the Gates*, an adventure-romance set in occupied France during World War II.

- 1974: The Filmakers Group purchased rights to *The Old Man*, Truman Nelson's portrait of John Brown as a great American revolutionary. Michael Wilson was to write the script and the film was planned for a 1976 release.

- 1977: Before *The House on Garibaldi Street* was made into a telefilm in 1979, Wise entertained the idea of directing the story of how Nazi war criminal Adolph Eichmann was captured in Argentina in 1960.

- 1980: Wise was to serve as executive producer of *Don't Stay After Dark*, to be directed by Bud Townsend and produced by Stan Musgrove.

- 1981: Writer Herbert Margolis and Wise developed an interracial love story to be set in Shanghai, tentatively called *Our Destiny*. Two years of negotiations with Chinese authorities who insisted on script changes ended with the project's cancellation.

- 1982: Wise worked on the thriller *In the Heat of Summer*, which he planned to shoot in black and white. The project later became *The Mean Season* [1985], directed by Phillip Borsos.

- 1985: Wise optioned *High Times, Hard Times*, the autobiography of singer Anita O'Day, and a biography of Mae West, the latter to star Bette Midler.

- 1986: Wise was announced as director and co-producer of a romantic comedy called *Going to the Chapel*.

- 1986: Wise and his *Star Trek—The Motion Picture* associate producer Jon Povill planned a film about Gary McGivern, a man convicted of killing a New York City police officer.

• 1986: The Cannon Group reunited Wise with former collaborators Saul Chaplin, Ernest Lehman and Michael Kidd for the film version of the stage musical *Zorba*. Anthony Quinn was slated to reprise his famous role opposite John Travolta, but months into pre-production, constant budget cuts convinced the filmmakers that it would be impossible to make the film as originally planned. Wise spent ten months on the project.

FILMS AS PRODUCER

In addition to the films that he both produced and directed, Wise produced two films by first-time directors—*The Sergeant* [1968] directed by John Flynn, and *The Baby Maker* [1970] directed by James Bridges.